INVESTIGATIVE
REPORTING
A Casebook

INVESTIGATIVE REPORTING
A Casebook

by
THOMAS PAWLICK

PUBLISHED BY
RICHARDS ROSEN
PRESS, INC.
NEW YORK

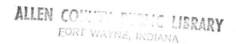
Published in 1982 by Richards Rosen Press, Inc.
29 East 21st Street, New York, N.Y. 10010

First Edition

Library of Congress Cataloging in Publication Data

Pawlick, Thomas.
 Investigative reporting.

  Summary: Examines the theory of investigative reporting, which includes planning,
researching, and writing a story for publication, and points out how to avoid the pitfalls
of libel and slander. Includes case histories
of investigative reporting.
  1. Reporters and reporting. [1. Reporters
and reporting] I. Title.
PN4781.P38   070.4'3   81–17897
ISBN 0–8239–0563–2   AACR2

To
Steve and Theresa Kennedy
and
Mary Frances Collins
of the *Westward*

ABOUT THE AUTHOR

Thomas Pawlick is a veteran journalist with more than sixteen years' experience writing and editing for newspapers, magazines, and wire services in the United States and Canada. Born in Detroit, Michigan, in 1941, he studied at Michigan State University, the Université de Poitiers in France, Marygrove College, and the University of Detroit, from which he received a bachelor of arts degree in 1965. He has worked as a reporter or an editor for the Detroit *News,* the Associated Press, Michigan's Booth Newspapers chain, and the Montreal *Gazette,* and he is currently employed as an associate editor of *Harrowsmith Magazine.* He is a member of the Centre for Investigative Journalism, whose *Annual Review* of the best investigative articles has featured his work. He has won the Canadian Ministry of State for Science and Technology National Journalism Award three times, in 1974, 1979, and 1980, and in 1976 he was awarded the U.S. National Conference of Christians and Jews Brotherhood Award for Journalism. His poetry and free-lance articles have appeared in publications throughout the U.S. and Canada, including the Chicago *Sun-Times,* Detroit *Free Press,* Montreal *Star, Chicago Journalism Review* and *Canadian Forum,* as well as in numerous literary magazines. A former high school teacher, he served for two years as training editor of the Montreal *Gazette,* responsible for the organization and implementation of the paper's intern program for journalism students. One of his students subsequently won the National Newspaper Award, Canada's highest journalism award, and a second received the Roland Michener Award for public service in journalism. Mr. Pawlick is married to the former Joanne Wolk and lives with her and their three children on a small farm in rural Canada.

CONTENTS

PREFACE

"There is no such thing as investigative journalism," a Detroit *News* editor once told me. "There is only good—or bad—reporting." The editor was at least partly right. All in-depth reporting is "investigative," in the sense that it tries to uncover all the facts and present as detailed and relevant an account of events as possible. If it does not do this, it is just plain slipshod work.

Nevertheless, to paraphrase one of the protagonists in Orwell's *Animal Farm,* some stories are more investigative than others, that is, they require more old-fashioned detective work than merely attending an event and recording it accurately in a notebook. To get these stories, a reporter must engage in sleuthing on a wholly different level of intensity than that called for by most news events. Such an effort demands method, specialized modes of procedure that must be learned before they can be practiced successfully.

This book is an attempt to describe the functional methods used by some working journalists, including the author, in gathering such stories. It is hoped that it will prove of practical use to other practitioners.

The need for responsible investigative reporting is crucial in any society, but especially in a modern democracy where an informed citizenry is essential to the governing process. Efforts to prevent the people from finding out the truth have become all too frequent of late and, whether covering government in Washington or any other legitimate object of the public interest, the journalist would do well to maintain a strong sense of his real relationship with those in power.

The following verse, quoted in the *Chicago Journalism Review,* describes it well:

> Press Conference.
> There is a pause, then flags.
> Gentlemen: (We rise)
> The playbill fills with sudden traps,
> Pomp, like a prize, walks into ambush.
> Hail to the chief.

PART ONE
THEORY

Chapter I

THE ELEMENTS

The city editor of the Montreal *Gazette,* Claude Arpin, held out a letter: "This is a real long shot, a missing person," he told the reporter. "I don't think you'll have much luck, but you may want to try it anyway."

The letter was from a woman in West Haverstraw, New York, and it really was a long shot.

"I'm writing you as a last resort, in hopes that the *Gazette* can help me find my father," the woman wrote. She added that she hadn't seen her father in twenty-seven years, didn't know his address—or even what country he might be in—didn't know whether he was working, at what, or if he was actually still alive.

All she had was his name and the fact that he had once lived in the Montreal suburb of Verdun. He didn't live in Verdun anymore, she said. She had been to Montreal several times in the past twenty-seven years, had gone to Verdun and found no trace of him.

She had searched the records at city hall, water tax records, electric utility billing records, everything. All in vain. "He would be over seventy years old now," she wrote. "You are my last hope of finding him before he dies."

"Do you want to try it?" the editor asked.

The reporter did. An hour later, he called the woman from West Haverstraw long-distance to tell her that he had found her father alive and well. She was overcome with joy.

"How did you do it?" the city editor asked, astounded.

"I looked him up in the phone book," said the reporter, and that was the truth. There was no one by the name given in the Montreal directory, but there was a vaguely similar name, with the same first initial, listed in Verdun. It turned out to be the long-lost father.

"One side of Dad's family always spelled the name differently than the other," explained the happy daughter. She had looked under both spellings herself during her trip to Verdun, but her father was apparently living somewhere else at the time and wasn't in that year's phone book. He had moved back to Verdun later, in time for the reporter's call.

"Tears of joy end 27-year separation," the November 1977 headline triumphed. The morning edition story ran on page one, above the fold, with a four-column photograph of father and daughter, both grinning.

3

Page 1 of the Montreal Gazette, *November 1977: The happy result of a missing persons investigation that paid off. The missing man's name and address were in the telephone directory.*

When the reporter came to work that afternoon he found a gallon bottle of wine sitting on his desk, with a note attached that said "thanks." It was signed by the woman from New York.

Investigative reporting?

Yes, the story was a classic example of it. Brief as it was, it combined all the basic elements of investigative journalism in microcosm. There was a question to be answered (where was the vanished man?), a public good to be served by answering it (the reunion of a long-separated family), and a good news story to be had. Finally, the man was located through a combination of the two elements central to all investigative reporting—elementary legwork and plain luck.

The fact that my "legwork" only involved opening the telephone book is irrelevant. A lot of stories come to nothing because reporters don't bother to open the phone book. Over luck, no one has much control, but where legwork is concerned there's no excuse for not doing it.

The research necessary to break an investigative story, however, is rarely so simple as it proved in the above case. Most of the time it's a lot more complicated, and complex problems require method to solve.

Every investigative reporter has his own way of doing things, his own personal bag of tricks. Some, like Bob Woodward and Carl Bernstein of Watergate fame, depend heavily on tipsters, on developing contacts who can channel information to them. Others emphasize documentation, file searches, and record-keeping.

Still others go the "cowboy" route, masquerading as suckers, potential victims of various con games, in order to draw out their quarry, or, like Montreal television reporter Brian McKenna, go looking for "points of tension." McKenna, who exposed a series of kickbacks and shady deals that led to millions of dollars in cost overruns at the 1976 Montreal Olympic Games, got the final bit of proof needed for his story by locating an in-law of one of those involved, who had a grudge to settle. The in-law, to get back at his wheeler-dealer relative, told McKenna all.

Freelancer Lynn McTaggart, whose 1975 New York *Daily News* story, "How I bought—and almost sold—a baby," exposed several black market baby adoption rackets, is a good example of the cowboy style. She posed first as an unwed mother and then as a prospective adoptive parent to get her information.

But the differences in style between reporters are differences in emphasis only. Woodward and Bernstein may have depended heavily on the mysterious informer known as "Deep Throat" to get the truth on Richard Nixon, but they had to dig through files as well. McTaggart, too, had to do her research before she started calling the baby brokers, and even the most thorough file-comber sooner or later has to interview those who wrote the documents he has found.

It's all part of the same picture, or rather the same jigsaw puzzle. So where does the reporter start? What steps should be followed to put all the pieces together?

There are at least eight steps essential to every investigative news story: (1) backgrounding; (2) planning; (3) stalking; (4) clinching it; (5) getting the reply; (6) writing it; (7) getting it published; and (8) following up.

Of course, some of these steps may be telescoped into each other in the course of an actual investigation. Others may appear almost painfully obvious. But the work that goes into each phase can be far from obvious, and ignoring any step can be dangerous.

Unfortunately beginners—and sometimes experienced reporters who are in a hurry—try to get by with skipping a step. Sometimes they get lucky, and it works. But more often the result is a botched job.

Chapter II

BACKGROUND AND PLANNING

The backgrounding phase of an investigation is often the most important. As Mao Tse-tung once put it: "In order to destroy an enemy, you must first know who he is."

Whether the reporter's starting point is the name of an individual or a company, the description of a racket or simply a hunch that a particular situation might bear looking into, the first place to go is the clippings file, or morgue, of the newspaper library and the reference books on the library shelves.

One consumer reporter actually starts with the set of law books—the Criminal and Civil Codes—that record the statutes of the state in which she works. She reads over the laws and tries to imagine ways to break them and get away with it. If she thinks of a good scheme, her logical assumption is that someone else has thought of it too and is doing it. All she has to do to get a good story is to start looking in the right places for someone with the same sort of devious mind as her own.

For all a reporter knows, however, the story that has suggested itself may already have been broken by his or her own paper or one of its competitors. There is nothing so disappointing as going through the labor of getting that big scoop only to find out it isn't a scoop at all, that somebody else did it a year ago. Checking the clippings insures against such a prospect.

Once it has been established that the potential story would be new, the clips can provide valuable leads. Every name, under every possible spelling, should be checked out and the subject file combed as well. Not every clip file is well enough organized to be cross-referenced.

After the clip file comes the trusty telephone book, including the *Yellow Pages,* and then the local city directory or street index. If the operators on the newspaper's switchboard have a copy of the Bell Telephone *Red Book,* it should be checked too.

Phone books, especially the *Yellow Pages,* are surprisingly rich sources of information. A company's *Yellow Pages* advertisement may list products or services it provides of which the reporter was not aware, or give addresses of all of the company's branch offices. Ads by competing firms, carried on the same page, provide a handy list of commercial rivals who may know a lot about how the first firm does business and be willing to talk about it.

The street index tells who a firm or an individual's neighbors are, who shares the same floor of the office building or apartment house, and who lives next door. The *Red Book* lists phone numbers in numerical order, with the subscriber's names in the opposite column. If all a reporter has to go on is a telephone number, the *Red Book* will provide the name that goes with it.

If the starting point is the name of a business or manufacturer, ask the paper's finance editor for information and check through his reference books: *Standard and Poor's, Barron's, Moody's,* and the other business directories. If the paper doesn't have them, the local public library certainly will.

These directories will tell who owns the company, who sits on its board, what it sells or makes, and whether it is a subsidiary of some larger firm. If the company sells common stock to the general public, its prospectus and annual report may be available at a local stockbroker's office, or obtainable by writing the company and asking for copies.

Also useful as a source of information on business firms is the U.S. Securities and Exchange Commission (SEC) annual *Directory of Companies Required to File Annual Reports,* which lists firms alphabetically and by industry classification. Any company listed in the directory will have a file at the SEC, from which information can be obtained by writing the SEC in Washington, D.C., or phoning the commission at (202) 755–4846.

The SEC is not the only government body charged with regulating commerce. Other federal, state (in Canada, provincial), and local government offices also keep files on businesses. In American states, the Secretary of State's offices keep a record of all corporations registered in a state, but the amount of information on file varies widely. In New York, for example, only the date of incorporation and the county in which the firm does business are recorded. In other states, officers and directors are listed, along with financial details.

City or county clerks' offices may also have information on file if the company does business in their area or requires a license.

In Canada, the federal Ministry of Consumer and Corporate Affairs in Ottawa and various provincial departments, such as Quebec's Department of Financial Institutions, keep records on corporations. As in the U.S., city and county clerks' offices in Canada frequently have valuable data on businesses in their bailiwick. Other good sources of information on businesses are the local Better Business Bureau, Chamber of

Commerce, real estate board, trade and business associations—even the fraud and bunco squads of the local police force.

Fertile Mine

Still another fertile mine of facts is Dun and Bradstreet, the credit rating service known and respected throughout the financial world. Officially, the D&B credit rating service is available only to firms that have a demonstrable business reason for knowing another firm's credit history. Normally, requests for such information are made by a company's comptroller or other financial executive.

If someone calls out of the blue, identifying himself as a nosy reporter, the D&B staff won't give him the time of day. Inquiries are easier to pursue if a reporter can persuade the newspaper's comptroller to make the request, but the comptroller may not be eager to do so. A D&B report costs about $50, and too many requests from a newspaper— even its financial officer—may make D&B suspicious.

Getting a D&B report may be well worth the trouble, however. The reports are veritable treasure troves of information, giving everything from the firm's financial structure to the arrest records, if any, of its executive officers. Of particular interest to D&B are histories of bankruptcy—especially fraudulent bankruptcy—in companies previously operated by the current executives. The information in these reports is generally reliable, although sometimes a bit out of date.

The U.S. Interstate Commerce Commission, Federal Reserve Board, and National Labor Relations Board also provide facts, as do the equivalent ministries in Canada's federal government. Even the tax returns of nonprofit foundations can be obtained through the Internal Revenue Service in the United States.

(Interpreting the financial statements and economic information obtained from such sources can, of course, be complicated for the average reporter, who may not know a ledger book from a roll of paper towels. Aid in deciphering what otherwise might look like so much gobbledygook can be gained by reading the layman's guide, "How to Read a Financial Statement," available free from Merrill, Lynch, Pierce, Fenner and Smith, Inc., of New York.)

Information on real estate ownership can be obtained in most U.S. states from the county Register of Deeds office, where deeds and contracts of sale involving land and buildings are kept on file. In Canada, the same kind of information is on record at local Land Registry offices. The municipal or county property, water, and school tax collection rolls, often on file in the same building as the deeds, list the names of those who are paying the taxes on a given piece of real estate.

If more complete information is sought, or the searcher suspects the true owner may be employing a "front man" as a taxpaying agent, it may be worthwhile to seek the help of a title search expert. Such an expert, usually a lawyer, can make sense of unfamiliar documents and ferret out the real ownership history of a lot or house. The expert, however, may charge a fee for this service.

Biographies of prominent persons and politicians can be found in *Who's Who* and in government manuals, such as the Canadian *Parliamentary Guide* or U.S. state government guides such as *The Michigan Manual* or *The Pennsylvania Manual.* The personal and political histories of U.S. Senators, Representatives, and state governors are detailed in *The Almanac of American Politics,* published by E. P. Dutton of New York. If the person being researched is a medical doctor, a lawyer, or an engineer, his background may be outlined in the files of a professional association for doctors, lawyers, or engineers. Sometimes these associations publish *Blue Books* or directories of members, listing their education, club memberships, and employers.

Getting a person's police record is sometimes difficult. In some states and Canadian provinces, such information can be made available only to police officers or law enforcement officials. Even in localities where it is legal to give out such information, police are often reluctant to do so.

This is where a friend with a badge can come in handy, especially one with whom the reporter is in a position to trade information he already has in return for the policeman's favor. If the locals won't cooperate, a friend on another force may be able to make the request. The author once obtained a criminal record on a Canadian suspect through a police officer in New York, who made the request by Teletype through his detective bureau.

As for information on government activities, the U.S. Freedom of Information Act of 1966, which has been amended several times in the years since it was framed, provides another very useful channel through which data can be garnered. The Act applies only to the executive branch of the U.S. federal government, and does not pertain to information about the legislative branch or state governments. Nevertheless, it is a godsend for reporters. Directions on how to request data under the Act are contained in *A Citizens' Guide on How to Use the Freedom of Information Act and the Privacy Act in Requesting Government Documents,* available from the Superintendent of Documents, U.S. Government Printing Office, Washington, D.C.

This list of sources, of course, is far from exhaustive. With a little enterprise, reporters will be able to add to it with sources of their own. But the idea of backgrounding, of learning as much as possible about a subject before launching an inquiry, is basic.

The first step in an investigation is the backgrounding phase. The reference books in a newspaper library are a rich source of material.

Define Objectives

Planning the actual investigation is a bit like planning a battle. The reporter, like a military officer, must define an objective, what the story is intended to reveal, and decide what steps to take to reach it.

It is sometimes helpful to sit down, ballpoint in hand, and make a written outline. The main facts already established during the background phase can be listed in one column, noting the source beside each fact. In a second column, facts that still must be established in order to prove the story's thesis can be listed, along with possible sources of information. The hard part comes next: deciding in precisely what order those still-untapped sources should be checked. This is a crucial question, on which the success of the investigation may depend.

Say the reporter receives an anonymous tip that a city councilman is involved in a real estate deal that would constitute a conflict of interest. The councilman is rumored to have a share in a plot of land in the path of a city development project—a project for which he voted—and will make a bundle if the city buys the lot. According to the clip files, the councilman is a former realtor who still maintains contact with several local development companies.

The reporter suspects the councilman tipped a developer crony to the city's plans before they were voted on in council and arranged for the developer to buy the lots through an intermediary, or front man. When the city takes over the land, the profits will be split three ways: one part for the front man, one for the developer, and one for the councilman.

To prove that happened, a reporter would want both documentary evidence and witnesses' statements. But witnesses get nervous. They may be dishonest themselves, or frightened, and if questioned too soon they may tip the councilman that somebody is checking up on him. Thus forewarned, he can take steps to hide or destroy any documents that might cause him trouble, warn his friends not to talk to newspeople, and, in the meanwhile, concoct a nice story to defend himself.

If he's aggressive enough, he may even threaten the paper with legal action before the hapless reporter's investigation has gotten off the ground. So where should the investigator start?

With the documents, of course. A piece of paper isn't going to tell anyone that a newsman or woman has read it. It is discreet. Jumpy witnesses can be saved for later, after the reporter has gathered a little more proof. In the case of the realtor/councilman, the reporter should first check the Register of Deeds or Land Registry Office, the property tax assessment rolls, or any other source of documents that might show who owns the lot in question and who owned it in the past. He may also refer to documents from the "round file," to be discussed in Chapter III.

Only after such sources of written documentation have been checked should the reporter move on to interviews with live witnesses. When the time does come to begin such personal contacts, the first interviews should focus on those farthest away from the core group of suspected conspirators. Even these peripheral witnesses should be approached cautiously. Spook a secretary in city hall and that secretary may run straight to the boss.

It helps to think of the suspected parties as being at the center of several concentric rings or circles. Probing should start at the outer rim of the target and work gradually in toward the bullseye. It should be done as prudently as possible, on the strength of whatever excuses the reporter can think of for asking questions *except* that he suspects something crooked is going on.

In an ideal investigation the suspect shouldn't even know that inquiries are being made until he is actually confronted, in the presence of a witness, with the evidence of his wrongdoing and asked to explain himself. Caught by surprise, he may blurt out a quote that will clinch the story for the writer—and cut the crook's throat.

That, of course, is the ideal. More than likely the quarry will be aware of the hunters only too soon. But why give them that advantage any sooner than necessary?

A reporter should keep such things in mind while planning an investigation. The steps of the inquiry should follow logically, building a case, until they reach the point where the suspect is fenced in by evidence.

A third column should be added to the reporter's written plan of action, numbering each step in its order of "safety," that is, its potential for spooking witnesses. Whenever possible the investigation should be carried out in that order. Doing this is the first step in learning the art of stalking.

Breaking a good investigative story is rarely the result of accident. It has to be planned. Without good planning, a journalist is no better than a bull in a china shop, blundering here and there and coming up with precious little to write under a by-line.

Chapter III

STALKING

The art of stalking cannot be taught. It is a talent, an ability that goes with a certain personality and frame of mind. A good investigative reporter has to be able to think logically, but more specifically in terms of puzzles. He or she must also have the sporting instinct—the love of an old-fashioned chase and a bulldog determination not to let go until the quarry is cornered.

If someone's personality is built that way, there is no more purely satisfying joy than the one he or she will feel when the big break comes at the end of a long, detailed inquiry and he can say, as a Detroit *News* reporter once shouted to a startled newsroom: "I've got the bastards!" It's a little like being drunk.

But having such a personality won't do much good if a reporter doesn't know how to use it. There are certain tools of the trade, and they take skill and knowledge to use.

Some of the most reliable tools include the telephone, the tape recorder, the garbage can, the interview, and the expertise of good contacts. Another tool, for lack of a better name, might be called reflection. It is something more than just sitting down and thinking about a problem. It's a certain *way* of thinking about a problem.

The telephone is a wonderful instrument, whose many facets are particularly appreciated by writers for the wire services, such as the Associated Press. AP writers, who rarely have time to get out of the office to cover a story, become adept at "working the phones," at keeping ahead of their competition with the help of Ma Bell.

Early in the game, they realize they can get there faster by phone than in a car, hitting their interview subjects by surprise and at all hours. They can contact two or three interview subjects at the same time, by using several extension lines, and thus prevent one source from telephoning the other to warn him that a reporter is snooping.

They learn the art of timing calls, of harassing via telephone, and of telephone "dirty tricks." One wire service reporter scored a beat on all his competitors by obtaining an interview by phone when the rest of the pack were actually on the scene.

A celebrity arrived at an airport, where reporters were waiting to question him, and was greeted by a page over the airport loudspeaker asking him to "come to the phone immediately." He walked right past the waiting reporters and answered the phone. It was the AP calling.

Another AP man, hearing about a shoot-out between bandits and police in a neighborhood on the other side of the city from his office, knew that if he tried to go to the scene by car the incident would be over before he arrived. He pulled out the city directory, looked up the names of the neighbors living next door to the shooting scene, and telephoned them. A woman, obviously scared stiff, answered and, in a quavering voice, described the drama as it unfolded outside her living room window. The reporter had an eyewitness description of the whole scene and never left his desk to get it.

The usefulness of the telephone is also apparent to the investigative reporter. One newswoman had been trying to swing an interview with a businessman for weeks, to no avail. One afternoon, leaving his office after once more being told "he's not in today," she noticed a note on the receptionist's desk advising the businessman to "please call Salt Lake City." The reporter wasted no time. She went to a pay phone outside, dialed the businessman's office, and when the receptionist answered said: "Long distance from Salt Lake City for Mister. . . ." giving the businessman's name. The man, who had been intending to call the Salt Lake City number anyway, decided to take the call and came on the line. Before he knew what was happening, the reporter he'd been trying so hard to avoid was interviewing him.

The telephone can also be used as a supplement to an in-person interview. Often a person being interviewed is reluctant to speak during a first encounter with a journalist, particularly an aggressive journalist whose strong personality comes across in conversation. Telephoned later for further detail, however, the same person may suddenly open up and talk freely. Whether it is the "safe distance" provided by speaking over the phone, compared to the "dangerous" situation of conversing face to face, or simply the fact that the reporter has become a familiar quantity by the time the second conversation begins, that subsequent telephone callback "for further details" has been known to work wonders.

Tape Recorders

Also a means of working occasional wonders is that little black box known to the French as *le magnetophone*—in English, the tape recorder. The use of this machine, which can provide a reporter with indisputable backup in case somebody denies having said something, also takes skill.

In face-to-face interviews, the mere sight of a turning tape reel can make subjects freeze solid. They get stage fright, stumble over their words, keep glancing at the recorder and losing their train of thought. Sometimes, realizing that their words are being absorbed for later verbatim playback, they lie, dissemble, hedge, hem and haw.

The wise journalist realizes this and compensates for it. At the beginning of the interview the recorder can be hauled out and placed in an off-to-the-side corner of a desk or table, while the reporter asks: "Would you mind if I record some of this later on, so I don't end up misquoting you?" If the reporter is careful not to turn the recorder on at this point, but to leave it as something to be used "later on," the person being interviewed will usually agree to be recorded. Subsequently, at a point in the talk where things start to get interesting, the journalist can quietly switch the machine on, preferably when his subject is looking the other way, and start recording.

This method allows the person being questioned to get used to the idea of being recorded gradually, while not fearing—at least at the outset—that he or she will say something unfortunate. By the time the conversation is going full blast and the subject has warmed to his topic, the soft click of the recorder going on may not even be noticed.

If the tape runs out in the middle of a crucial conversation, it's best not to stop to change the spool or cassette. Let the subject think it's still running, so he won't be tempted to retract his statements later, and keep the momentum of the conversation going. No reporter should depend entirely on the tape recorder, anyway. The trusty pen and notebook should always be in use as a backup.

After those key quotes are safely noted in the reporter's pad, he can wait for a less crucial point in the interview and then calmly change the spool. If the journalist feels he absolutely must have the material on tape, he can at this point ask the original questions over again, in slightly different words, and record the repeated, and probably more detailed, second reply. The person being interviewed may think the reporter a bit repetitive but won't know that those first key quotes never went on tape.

With the aid of a phone jack attachment, the tape recorder can also be tuned in to record a telephone conversation. In some U.S. states and Canadian provinces recording a phone conversation is frowned on by the law unless the person being taped is warned in advance that he is being recorded. Other jurisdictions require a beeper tone to sound every few seconds on the tape track. It is a good idea, before buying a phone jack, to check the local privacy and wiretapping laws and regulations. It would be an unpleasant turnabout for an investigation to end with the reporter being charged.

In many courts, tape recordings are still not admissible in evidence in a libel trial, the judges apparently believing that these "newfangled, magical gadgets" called tape recorders are not trustworthy. In such

A tape recorder attached to the telephone by means of a phone jack provides an accurate record of what was said during an interview. Some courts do not admit tape recordings in evidence, and a careful reporter will also take written notes or ask a friend to listen in on an extension line.

17

circumstances, a reporter's only hope of defending the accuracy of a quote is to offer written notes or the testimony of a live witness to the conversation at issue, or both.

It is a good practice, when interviewing a person who may sue, to arrange to have a colleague listen in on an extension phone line and take notes. The reporter's notes and those of his colleague will gain more credence from a court if they are taken down in shorthand, but any kind of notes are better than none. In a legal action, the reporter and his colleague can both provide live verbal testimony and back it up with their respective notes, written separately in their own handwriting.

Depending on the length of its microphone cord, the tape recorder can serve all sorts of useful—and unexpected—purposes. One city hall reporter in a small Michigan city was frustrated, for example, at the tendency of several city council committees to hold closed-door meetings to which the press was refused access. One night, as still another tight-lipped council committee filed out of the council chamber into a private room for an in camera consultation, she had a brainstorm.

Clutching her tape recorder, which had a long mike cord, the reporter went upstairs to the room above the secret meeting room. She found the heating duct, unscrewed its grate with the help of a coin, and dropped the microphone down inside the chute until it slid to a halt just inside the heating grate in the room downstairs. She flipped her recorder on and taped the whole proceeding. When it ended, she fished her mike back up, screwed the grate back in place, and went back to the paper.

The next day a verbatim account of the secret meeting was carried on page three of the paper. The council committee members were shocked, believing one of their members had leaked the story, and became even angrier when the same thing happened a month later after another secret meeting. Finally, unable to discover the traitor in their midst, they gave up holding secret meetings.

Round File Mata Hari

Still another useful tool is the humble "round file," or garbage can, which is almost as good as having a Mata Hari in the enemy's camp. The trash barrel may not have a perfume like that of the famous World War I spy, but it gathers as many secrets.

People throw all kinds of things out in their trash: bills and invoices, confidential letters, spoiled carbons of business contracts, scrap-paper notes jotted while on the telephone, old phone bills listing every call they've made over the past months (with the number and toll charges), in short, anything and everything.

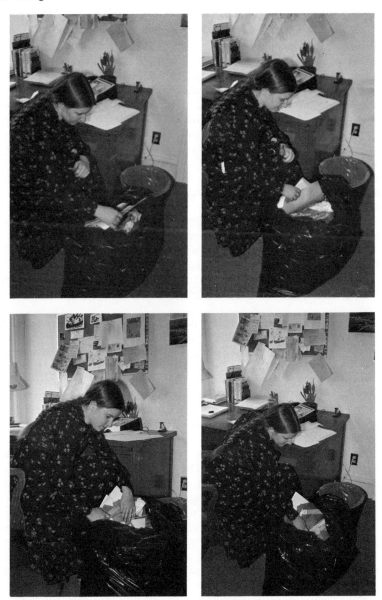

Documents thrown out in home or office rubbish are often of great value to an investigator who takes the trouble to acquire them. Here, a reporter sifts through "the round file" in hopes of finding new information.

Frequently, the documents in question have been torn into pieces that must be painstakingly reassembled, jigsaw-puzzle fashion, with the aid of a roll of Scotch tape. They are also often smeared with bacon grease, coffee grounds, banana peels, and eggshells, to name only a few of the more unsavory surprises found in this manner. In one case, a letter that helped incriminate a crook was crumpled inside a baby's used diaper. Needless to say, this sort of source calls for a strong stomach, but the rewards are worth it.

One crooked Montreal doctor, whose activities were an open book to investigators who "read" his trash every week, got a bit paranoid when his secrets began to come out. He thought his office had been electronically bugged and wrote a notice to his staff warning them not to discuss confidential deals aloud but to write everything down in notes to one another.

Both his warning and the staff's obedient notes showed up later in his trash barrel, like little gifts from the goddess of investigators.

All a reporter has to do to latch onto such rich hauls of information is to call the city public works department and ask on what days and at what times trash is picked up on the block where the suspect party lives or does business. Get there five minutes before the garbage truck, and a gem may be waiting.

Though bizarre, such raids are not illegal. Once put out in the trash, property is considered legally abandoned, so no theft is involved. If the trash is set out in a public alley, or by a public sidewalk, the reporter is not trespassing if he grabs it.

The only risk involved in snatching trash is that the suspect will see the reporter doing it and become suspicious. This is always a risk in summer, when both morning and evening trash pickups take place in broad daylight. In winter, at least, the garbage picker's antics can be covered by darkness.

Another difficulty presents itself when the suspect's home or office is located in a high-rise office building or apartment house. On rubbish day, hundreds of bags are set out on the street for pickup, and finding the suspect's would be like looking for a broken eggshell in a haystack, so to speak. The problem can be solved by locating the floor on which the suspect lives or works. The cleaning staff gather all of the trash from each floor near an elevator or stairway before taking it down to the street. Go to the elevator or trash closet on the floor in question before the garbage is carried down and the looked-for bags will be waiting.

Other journalists, watching the investigative reporter sift through his smelly swag, pulling bits and pieces of paper out of the mess like diamonds from the ore of a mine, may think the poor chap has at last slipped over the edge. But they will not be the one whose by-line is carried above a page one exposé two weeks later. The grimy-handed garbage picker's name will be on the story.

Yet another useful tool is the face-to-face interview. Its requirements are not identical to those of the telephone interview, and, like each of the other tools of research, it demands a good deal of skill to be properly employed.

In an "open" interview, in which the subject knows his questioner is a reporter taking notes, the basic requisite is to gain the subject's confidence and put him or her at ease. In a "closed" interview, in which the subject is unaware that the person questioning him is a reporter, the goal is the same, but with a twist. The reporter, posing as a potential con-game victim or would-be partner in crime, must convince his interlocutor that he is talking either to a sucker or to another crook. The reporter, in other words, must con the con man (or woman).

Whether open or closed, a good interview should move to its main point gradually, obliquely, whenever possible. The reporter's questions should be framed in such a way that the really key questions don't appear to be key questions to the person being interviewed.

Ideally, the answer a reporter has been striving for should come in an aside, as an offhand answer to an offhand remark. Immediately after getting it, the reporter should switch the conversation to something else. The game of getting a crook to hang himself is like a shell game— now you see it, now you don't.

But the finer points of interviewing are best learned through experience and example. The case histories discussed in subsequent chapters will provide closer insight.

The last two tools listed previously were expert contacts and the art of reflection.

Every newspaper has its own private army of experts. If a business is being investigated, the paper's business section editors and its executive staff (remember that comptroller?) can help.

If a suspect's criminal record is needed, the paper's police reporters, especially its organized crime specialist, can lend a hand. Every specialty department, from the science page staff to the outdoor sports columnist, can provide leads and help put information into its proper context. The writer may have to share a by-line with someone if the amount of information gleaned is substantial, but if the story is good enough, why be an egotist?

Contacts outside the paper's staff must be approached with considerably more caution. An outside expert is more likely than a journalist's fellow reporters to blab to a confrere that a newspaper reporter has been asking questions and hence is a greater risk to story security. An outside expert, say a chemist at a local university, may also have

The personal interview is a key part of almost every story and must be conducted with skill and sensitivity. The reporter's goal is always to set his interview subject at ease while gaining his or her confidence.

22

friends on the staff of an opposition paper and be tempted to tip them to the good story they're missing.

Expert advice, however, is frequently so valuable as to make it worth the risk. Take it, but take it carefully.

Everyone a reporter interviews, on any story, may be able to help in some future inquiry. When a good contact is made—especially if the contact is a police officer—the reporter should deal fairly and honestly with him and keep renewing the contact from time to time. Everyone, as the Beatles succinctly put it, "needs a little help from his friends."

As for reflection, it is a process difficult to put into words. Familiarity with the basic concepts of Japanese Zen Buddhism might help to understand it.

Throughout an investigation a reporter's conscious mind is constantly working in a logical pattern, trying to put bits and pieces together, to synthesize. But sometimes there are too many bits, and the investigator's circuits get overloaded. He or she just can't seem to find where that last jigsaw piece fits.

It's time for reflection, which is not a logical thing at all.

The best thing to do is to sit down in some quiet place, away from interruptions, and try to focus on the *whole* story. Not its details, not their logical progression, but the story overall, as an entity in itself. The reporter should try to feel all of its separate events as one event, one reality. Then hold it.

Let that reality do the rest.

It is amazing how reality can speak to a person who listens, even when it isn't asked. It happened to the author once in an airplane, flying back from an apparently unsuccessful series of interviews in a distant city. Sitting there in the economy-class seat, looking out at the tops of the clouds below the Boeing jet, I *felt* the person who had the answer and exactly how to approach him.

When the plane landed, a phone call from a booth at the airport located the man in question and, as if prodded by some unseen force, he spilled everything.

The story, its author whistling happily as he typed, was written the same night and appeared on page one the next day. A Zen monk would make a very good detective.

One more piece of equipment should be mentioned in any discussion of tools: the camera. Most large newspapers employ staff photographers who relieve reporters of the burden of obtaining "art" for their stories, but weekly, magazine, and freelance writers who do not have access to this kind of professional help may have to take their own pictures. Even a reporter lucky enough to work with a staff photographer cannot afford to become lazy, adopting a "let the photo expert take care of it" attitude. Too many opportunities can be lost that way.

An investigative reporter should be able to see the possibilities for photography in a story and either take good photos himself or suggest possible shots to his professional partner. For example, one reporter working on an investigation of illegal chemical waste disposal found that trucks carrying toxic chemicals from a local factory were driving out to a rural area at night and dumping their poisonous cargo in a farmer's field. He helped his photographer rig a strobe light at the site and when the trucks came took a flash photo of the dumpers in action. The photo showed the startled face of one driver and the license plate number of a truck, and when it was published it enabled police to find and arrest the culprit. The driver and the trucking company he worked for both paid fines for illegal dumping.

As readers and reporters both know, a single picture can sometimes be worth more than a hundred pages of printed copy.

Chapter IV

CLINCHER AND REPLY

Clinching an investigation and getting the suspect's reply are often simultaneous events, if not the same event. They represent the climax of the reporter's effort, though not yet its denouement.

For a police officer investigating a crime, an inquiry climaxes when the officer establishes sufficient proof to make an arrest and brings the suspect in for a formal interrogation and statement at the police station. For a reporter, the same thing occurs when enough proof has been gathered to print the story without being open to a libel suit and the suspect is approached formally for comment on the story's charges.

Deciding when enough evidence has been gathered to clinch the story and print it without fear of lawsuits can pose some difficult problems. The reporter and his or her editors must consider not only what might happen if the person written about takes them into a court of law, but also how the story might fare in the court of public opinion.

For example, if a Washington newspaper had discovered that former U.S. Vice President Spiro Agnew was being investigated for income tax evasion during the period when Agnew was making his famous speeches against the "effete snobs" of the press, it might have decided not to print the story right away. Coming immediately in the wake of an attack by Agnew on the press, a news story hinting at the Vice President's dishonesty would have looked like mere sour grapes, an attempt to smear a press critic. It would have been wiser for the paper to wait until there was a lull in Agnew's virulent attacks, a period of quiet during which his name was absent from page one. The tax evasion story then would have a greater chance of being accepted at face value.

Such political considerations must play a part in deciding how and when to break a major investigative story. Unquestionably, however, the main consideration in most stories will be the legal aspect. It is here that the good judgment of both the reporter and the editors, as well as the ability of any libel lawyer consulted by the paper, must come into play.

The best defense against charges of libel, as a later chapter will explain more fully, is the truth. If the reporter can prove that what a story

25

stated was, indeed, factual and that in stating it his aim was not to hurt anyone but to inform the public, most libel suits against the reporter will fail. The reporter, then, has to be able to prove that what the story states is true.

Written documents that can be authenticated and live witnesses whose word the court is likely to accept are the best evidence a reporter can offer. Many newsmen follow the "Rule of Two Sources," namely that each statement in a story that could be attacked in court should be backed by two written documents, two live witnesses, or one of each.

If neither documents nor witnesses can be found to back up a controversial phrase or quote, it's best to leave it out—or hold off on printing the story until the needed proof can be gathered. Police officers face the same requirement. If they arrest someone without sufficient proof to make a case, they may be forced by the court to release their suspect—who may then turn around and sue the police for false arrest.

Sometimes, of course, both policemen and newspapers break the rules. Circumstances may be such that it seems worthwhile to take a chance and bluff the suspect. During the Watergate investigations of the Nixon Presidency, reporters for the Washington *Post,* the Los Angeles *Times,* and other publications almost routinely ran stories incriminating administration figures and based entirely on anonymous sources. Each time they did so they were courting a libel suit but correctly judged that the politicians involved would avoid legal action in order to avoid drawing still more attention to themselves and spurring more publicity of their misdeeds.

The Reply

Getting the subject of an investigative story to comment on the charges it contains also requires judgment and timing. Frequently, this stage of an investigation may bring additional facts to light, making the story that much richer, or reveal previously ignored points that might have gotten the reporter in trouble. Taking the time to get the reply is also necessary for basic fair play. Anyone who is accused of wrongdoing—from a Mafia don to the smallest of small-time con men—should be given the chance to defend himself, even if that defense should amount to no more than a terse "no comment."

The final confrontation between reporter and suspect should take place in front of witnesses, so that the person being interviewed will not be able later to deny what was said. It should also be tape-recorded, if possible, or at least recorded in the reporter's notes. The ideal situation is for the suspect to be alone—without witnesses favorable to him—while the reporter has at least one witness, such as a staff photographer, at his side, listening and prepared to testify in favor of the paper.

If a telephone interview is involved, the reporter's witness can listen in on the conversation on an extension line.

As already mentioned, the subject of an ideal investigation won't know that he or she is being investigated until the last minute, thus giving the journalist the advantage of surprise. Even if such an ideal situation does not exist, some element of surprise can still be obtained. If all of the reporter's previous interviews have been done during business hours, for example, he may surprise the suspect by calling him at home after business hours. The change in pattern may be just sufficient to throw the suspect off, catching him in a moment of relaxation when he is unprepared to speak and lacks access to notes or files kept at the office. Any amount of surprise is better than none.

The worst thing a newsman or woman can do is to call a suspect, tell him in so many words, "I'm coming over later to ask you if you are a crook," and then make the advertised visit on time. The suspect, in the gratuitously provided breathing space, may cover his tracks so well that a bloodhound can't find them. At the very least, the subsequent interview will likely net nothing of value to add to the impending story.

In the interview itself, the reporter may either take a sneaky approach, working the key questions into the conversation obliquely, or hit his suspect squarely between the eyes with the hard evidence and hard questions. Which approach to use in a given situation depends on the personality of the suspect and the nature of the evidence.

The goal is to get the suspect to further incriminate himself, and others where applicable, by blurting out the truth.

Sometimes the truth blurted out may not be what the reporter expected, but it should be sought nevertheless. It is possible that the journalist may have missed something important in his inquiry and that the person being confronted is in reality innocent. A Canadian freelance writer once found this out to his chagrin.

He had written an exposé of a provincial politician, charging that the politician held shares in a company that had been awarded a government contract, a classic conflict-of-interest story. Unfortunately, the corporate stock ownership records on which his story was based were out of date. As it turned out, the politician had sold his stock in the company after his election and at the time the contract was awarded had no connection with the firm. If the freelancer had phoned the politician and asked him about his connections with the company before publishing the story, he would have discovered the facts.

He did not phone.

When the story came out, he was forced to retract publicly what he had written and apologize to the politician. He was censured by the provincial press council, to boot. It was an altogether embarrassing experience, which the sadder but wiser reporter vowed never to repeat.

He is still doing investigative work, currently working for the news department of a major television network, but he is careful always to call anyone he investigates for their side of the story before broadcasting a word.

Other confrontations with the subjects of an inquiry have proven more pleasant for the reporters involved. For example Brit Hume, an associate of syndicated columnist Jack Anderson, was assigned to confront Washington lobbyist Dita Beard with documentary evidence that executives of International Telephone and Telegraph (ITT) had had suspicious dealings with the executives of the Republican Party and the Nixon administration in 1972.

When Hume presented the incriminating memo to Beard in her office, the ITT lobbyist openly admitted having written it and, for reasons known only to herself, indulged in a verbal attack on several other ITT executives. Her comments provided more copy for the subsequent Anderson column, which eventually led to the exposure of a major government scandal.

Former White House aide John Dean, implicated early in the Watergate investigations, turned on his former associates and blurted out all kinds of political secrets. His actions were typical of many persons when confronted with evidence of wrongdoing. In an effort to divert the spotlight from themselves, they try to turn it on someone else. This can and does work to the reporter's advantage.

Feeling satisfied with the strength of the evidence gathered and obtaining the suspect's comments on it are akin to the arrest and confession (or denial of guilt) phase in a police case. But the reporter's job isn't over yet.

The journalist's "legal brief"—his story—must still be written, published, and scrutinized in the court of public opinion and a verdict must be rendered.

Chapter V

WRITING, PUBLISHING, AND FOLLOW-UP

Style is an important factor in writing the investigative story, for the obvious reason that the more colorful and easy to read an article is, the more readers will be likely to read it through to the end. Equally important to an article's success, however, are logical organization and the deliberate use of what might be called "legal understatement."

Like any news story, an investigative article can be introduced with either a feature lead focused on some colorful or unusual incident or personality, or a "straight news lead" that bluntly summarizes the story's main points prior to examining each of the points in detail. The opening chapter of this book, describing the Montreal reporter's missing-person search, is an example of a feature lead, whereas the first paragraph of this chapter is a straight news summary of points developed in the subsequent copy. Usually a combination of the two types of leads is used in writing an investigative story, thus ensuring both that reader interest is stirred and that the story's main points are recounted somewhere near the beginning of the article.

A common device is to describe one of the story's key personalities— the bad guy or one of his victims—in action, then, after four or five paragraphs of such description, to break in with a summary of what those actions mean. The summary paragraph is frequently followed by a series of "bullet grafs"—paragraphs set off from the copy by large-type dots—stating each of the points the paper's or magazine's investigation has turned up. Here are two examples:

MIDDLETOWN, Pa.—Sixteen months after the Three Mile Island accident, a second major failure has emerged here—the inability of the federal and Pennsylvania state governments to respond to the worst emergency in the history of American nuclear power.

A three-month inquiry by *The News American* into the role government played at Three Mile Island after the nuclear emergency in March 1979 has established that:

• Federal and state officials concede they do not know precisely how much radiation escaped the plant during the emergency, since they did not have adequate monitoring equipment on hand when the accident occurred.

• Two independent studies have concluded that the amount of radioactive

iodine released into the atmosphere was greater—by 32 times in the case
of one test—than previously reported by federal officials . . . etc.

That story, published in the Baltimore *News American,* begins with
a two-paragraph straight news lead, followed by a series of bullet grafs.
The following exerpt from the Canadian-based *Harrowsmith Magazine*
shows a typical feature lead with a concluding summary paragraph:

> "Put yourself out for Leo!" urged one of the campaign mobilizing slogans
> in the 1977 election campaign of Ontario Minister of Northern Affairs Leo
> Bernier.
>
> One man who did just that was Benjamin Ratuski, prominent businessman
> from the town of Keewatin, population 2,112. As the Tory minister's cam-
> paign manager, he helped get out the vote in the sprawling, 64,500-square-
> mile northern riding Bernier calls home, doing everything from haranguing
> the Kenora faithful at the candidate's hat-in-the-ring rally to helping organize
> a "Bernier Day" fish fry at Eagle River.
>
> Standing next to the victorious Bernier, a pleased Ratuski smiled for the
> election night cameras as a Kenora *Daily Miner and News* photographer
> snapped the pair's picture for a page one election results story.
>
> Ratuski's satisfaction was understandable; according to Bernier, the two
> men have been "close friends for many years." Indian leaders in the Lake
> of the Woods region, however, see Ratuski's satisfaction in a different light.
> Publicly, privately and in little-publicized briefs to the government they sug-
> gest that Ben Ratuski's company—Shoal Lake Wild Rice Ltd.—is receiving
> preferential treatment from the provincial government in which Bernier is
> a leading figure.

An investigative story, as noted previously, is similar to a lawyer's
legal brief. It must present the evidence supporting whatever charges
are being made in a logical, step-by-step manner. Haphazard story con-
struction, with points of various significance being spotted all over the
story in no particular order and the evidence backing up each point
separated from it by extraneous material, will not only confuse the
readers but may also confuse the judge at a libel trial, resulting in a
ruling against the story's author.

The most common form of organization is to follow the order of
the bullet grafs, expanding on each point in the main part of the article
in the same sequence that the bullet grafs were listed. The most important points are discussed first, less important or incidental points afterward. All the evidence supporting a particular point is usually stated
immediately after the point has been introduced, rather than being
buried in some obscure part of the story later on.

As for "legal understatement," this is a journalistic description of
the practice of letting facts speak for themselves, without embellishment,

and allowing the reader to draw his or her own conclusions. For example, a story might say that a politician has a stock interest in a firm doing business with the government but stop short of actually saying that this is a conflict of interest. It is better to let the reader, once presented with the facts, draw that conclusion for himself.

It is also better, in writing investigative stories, to avoid the use of adjectives whenever possible. Adjectives are treacherous things, which can easily get an unsuspecting reporter in trouble with a judge. "Swarthy," "scowling," "gruff-voiced" villains have a tendency to snap back at writers who describe them so unflatteringly, easily convincing courts in libel cases that the reporter was out to get them for spiteful or malicious reasons.

A culprit described simply as "businessman Alfonse Capone," however, is less likely to be able to prove bias on the part of his biographer.

Readers are also more likely to be convinced of the reliability of a reporter's facts if those facts are recounted in a calm, deliberate way, rather than in the strident, hysterical tone of the angry fanatic or of the old-time Yellow Press. Color, even humor, can be included in an investigative story to give it life and interest, but the writer should be careful never to overdo it. Writing a report in the wrong way can be worse than not writing it at all.

Getting It Published

Once the story is written, the next step is to persuade the newspaper or magazine involved to publish it—a task that is not always easy. Unfortunately, not all newsmen are dedicated to the truth or feel any special responsibility to their reading public. Some upper-echelon editors and executives, particularly those who have not come up through the reporters' ranks, are more interested in playing it safe, in not rocking the boat, than in getting the facts before the public. Forever "running scared" of libel suits, they avoid controversy like the plague and regard reporters who write controversial stories as dangerous wild men to be gagged—or fired—at all costs.

Tom Blackburn, former editor of the now-defunct *A.D. Magazine,* once described such a situation as "letting the accountants edit the newspaper." The description was, if anything, unfair to accountants, whose stereotype image as milktoasts is often undeserved. The idea that it is bad to allow a spirit of fear and hesitation to dominate editorial news judgment, however, was bang on. Such a spirit kills good journalism.

Equally deadly is the influence of publishers and managing editors who allow their support of or personal friendships with politicians, corporate dons, or others to color their news judgment. All too often, a good investigative story may be killed, not because it isn't true, but because it runs against the bias of a paper's upper management.

Perhaps the most difficult thing for a serious investigative reporter to swallow, however, is having a good story die because it violates the rules of "formula journalism." Formula journalism is similar in concept to formula radio, an idea that gained prominence in the broadcasting industry back in the early 1950's and eventually came to totally dominate AM radio in North America.

The purpose of the formula was to allow a radio station to cut its staff—and thus its salary overhead—to the bare minimum, to cut its production costs, and despite these economies still manage to attract the largest possible number of listeners. The formula used to accomplish this is now standard on virtually all AM radio stations: a half hour of "top ten" disc jockey tunes followed by a five-minute "news split" during which news headlines—but no details—are read. The sequence music/news split/music/news split is repeated all day. It is directed at the "lowest common denominator" of the mass audience and never varies.

A similar though slightly more complex pattern has been developed for newspapers, and many publishers, including New York *Post* owner Rupert Murdoch, have been accused of adopting it as their guide. Basically, it consists in writing short, punchy stories aimed at shocking, flattering, titillating, or arousing the greed of the readers. Stories whose aim is to inform are considered superfluous. It is the old tabloid formula of the 1930's Yellow Press revived, but without the vigor and sporting atmosphere that was present in the old days. Only the more shocking of investigative stories—those revealing, for example, that the mayor is a sex maniac or an ax murderer—are likely to get into print. Longer, carefully researched articles dealing with serious questions of public policy are considered boring or downbeat and are ignored.

The author once had to deal with an editor who believed in formula journalism. The editor in question regarded in-depth inquiries as a waste of manpower and the stories they produced as fit only for an "elite readership." He once ordered a halt to an investigation that had found evidence that a New Jersey Mafia family had gained indirect financial control of a major industry in his city on grounds that the "package would be long and boring." In his vocabulary, stories were all "packages" to be sold to the public.

Faced with such obtuseness on the part of his or her editors, the investigative reporter must be ready to wage a battle—sometimes longer and more wearying than was the business of gathering the story in the first place—to get an article published. It helps to have a few tricks up one's sleeve when the battle begins.

If the editors in question are libel-shy, a reporter can often outflank them by taking his story to the paper's libel lawyer for review *before* handing it in at the city desk. If the lawyer looks it over and says it is safe to publish, the timid editors' favorite excuse for not using controversial articles is demolished before they can employ it. (Handing a story over to the editor first, naively assuming that the editor will show it to the lawyer, could be a mistake. Often, if a story looks doubtful, a frightened editor won't bother with a legal review but will simply kill it on his own authority.)

Using the paper's libel lawyer as a wedge in this way presupposes, of course, that the reporter and attorney have a good working relationship and respect each other, and that the lawyer will not turn around and report everything the journalist told him to his editors. It also presupposes that the editors will not resent the reporter's bypassing them in this way, going over their heads to an expert.

If an editor with the authority to kill a story is known to be biased against the viewpoint presented in an article, the wise investigative reporter will try to work around him. For example, if the city editor would likely kill a story or rewrite it beyond recognition because it conflicts with his personal prejudices, the reporter might hold the story back for a weekend edition, over which the Sunday editor has jurisdiction. The reporter might also hold the story back until the city editor is on vacation and an assistant city editor with more compatible views is sitting in. If all else fails, he can try turning the story in right at deadline, when everyone is in a frantic rush and the editor may not have time to give it a close reading.

Ingenuity is a salient quality in a reporter.

When dealing with the formula journalist, reporters must often stretch their imagination to seek out a way to make the story seem splashy. Sometimes the splashy angle need only be emphasized in verbally describing the article to the formula editor, who will approve it and leave the actual editing or rewriting to the copy desk. The written version of the story can then be completed in a responsible manner.

However, if the formula journalism fan insists that the story actually be written in a splashy, irresponsible way, the reporter may have to grit his teeth and let it die rather than consciously distort the truth.

He may also decide to freelance the article to another publication, under his own by-line or a pen name. As a last resort, he may phone a rival reporter on another paper and give the information to him. If the reporter's own paper has had first crack at the story and won't use it, better that the opposition should have it than no one at all.

This, of course, brings up a question of journalistic ethics. Generally speaking, if a reporter is employed full-time at a newspaper or magazine it is considered not only unethical but a firing offense to publish an article in a competing newspaper or magazine. The full-time reporter can normally only freelance to a noncompeting publication. By non-competing most editors mean a newspaper in another city, state, or province.

However, if a reporter has clearly found information of real importance of which the public should be aware and his paper refuses to publish it, a higher good than mere employee loyalty may be at stake. Many investigative reporters have contacts on rival newspapers, where they can freelance a story under a pen name or give the information to another writer when they are faced with difficulties at their own paper. In the late 1960's and early 70's, the author routinely freelanced stories refused by his own employers to a weekly paper in Detroit. Often they ran with no by-line.

While working for a Detroit daily in the 1960's, editor Tom Blackburn, mentioned earlier, used to sneak editorials dissenting from the publisher's viewpoint into the paper via the book review column. "They [the newspaper's upper management] never read books anyway; they'll never notice it," Blackburn theorized. He was right. They never did notice, but a lot of readers did.

The truth has a way of leaking through barriers set up against it, especially if the reporter who has discovered it makes a few holes in the barricades to help it along.

Even if the paper's management presents no objection to using an investigative article, its effects can still be sabotaged by those friendly, usually competent but sometimes maddening people in the "back shop," the printers and paste-up personnel in the composing room. It can also be destroyed by the editors working the copy desk and the headline writer who writes the line the readers always see first.

The author was once threatened with a lawsuit because two key paragraphs in a story were cut out for space reasons in the composing room. It was an editor, not a printer, who decided that those two paragraphs had to go, but similar situations have stemmed from the mere careless flick of a paste-up knife or the malfunctioning of a typesetting computer.

Another reporter faced a lawsuit because the copy editor who wrote the headline for his story went further than the reporter had. Where the story had only implied that a certain prominent businessman was a crook, the head said it outright.

Unless a reporter has unusual confidence in his co-workers, he will do well to hang around after his own deadline to see what happens to a dicey story. This may irritate the copy desk, or make the city editor laugh, but it could also save the reporter's job or reputation someday. After several bad experiences, a seasoned investigative journalist may never leave the newsroom when an important story is being edited or typeset. He will wait until the first edition comes off the press and he has the printed, error-free story in his hands before going home.

Whenever possible, the reporter should amble into the composing room and loiter there, watching the paste-up process. As long as editorial employees don't physically touch the type or the paste-up boards, but keep their hands clasped inoffensively behind their backs, the printers' union won't mind. It's a good way to get to know the printers as individuals, to make friends who may later be of value. A friendly printer won't mind making a correction suggested by his reporter pal; an unfriendly one will ignore everything the reporter says.

Follow-up

The last step in the story process is the follow-up. It is every bit as important in producing results as the story itself.

Even the splashiest of exposés may prompt no official remedial action, or even response from the readers, if it dies after one day on page one. If a reporter really wants to rectify the problems his story has revealed, he has to keep the story moving, to keep it in the readers' minds where they will mull it over and maybe write a letter to the editor or to their Congressman.

That's what makes government officials react. No matter how shocking the abuses exposed by an article might be, any plan to do something about them may be banished to limbo with amazing speed unless the politicians think the voters are truly upset and want action.

The standard way to keep a story moving, at least on the second day, is to write a follow-up article reporting what steps the officials concerned are taking in light of the original story's revelations. Often they will be doing nothing, which is a story in itself. Call the officials, pester them. Get their quotes and keep the typewriter clicking. Without at least a second-day follow story, no investigative article is complete.

Another technique employed by reporters is to hold back some secondary pieces of information when writing the first article, saving them for use in another story the following day. Sometimes, if the situation being discussed is complex and interesting enough to warrant it, the story can be broken up into several parts and run on three or four successive days as a series. An occasional good exposé can be stretched out over a whole week, making it almost impossible for rival newspapers or broadcast stations to avoid going after it themselves, out of embarrassment. Their own readers or listeners, if the competition's story runs long enough, will eventually begin phoning or writing them to ask why *they* haven't reported it.

After the initial flap has died down, the reporter can come back to the story again in two or three weeks' time and do a "progress report."

Whatever method is used, the basic idea is to keep the story in the paper as long as possible—or until somebody in authority finally decides to correct the problem.

All of the investigative steps described so far have been reduced to their basic elements and defined in the abstract. This is fine as far as mere theory goes, but to really grasp the tricks of any trade the apprentice must see them in actual practice and eventually try them out himself.

The following case histories, every one of them true, may help give what has so far been a largely hypothetical exposition a bit more substance. They are drawn mainly from the author's own experience, mistakes and blunders included, in hopes that they may prove instructive.

PART TWO
PRACTICE

Chapter VI

THE BABY BROKERS

Black market adoptions, in which babies born to unmarried girls are sold to childless married couples for prices ranging as high as several thousand dollars, constitute one of the darkest chapters in the ongoing history of North American criminality.

Unlike adoptions arranged through legitimate government-run or private charitable organizations, which charge only a nominal administrative fee for their services and take great care to look after the health and welfare of the mother, child, and carefully screened adoptive parents, black market adoptions are fraught with cruelty and excesses born of irresponsible greed.

Profit, not the welfare of those concerned, is the motive at work in these exchanges. The health of the natural mother and child, the feelings of the adoptive parents, rules of confidentiality, screening to detect adoptive parents who are unfit to care for children—all of these factors are ignored. The black market brokers will sell any child to anyone under any circumstances, providing the price is right. To them a living human baby has no more importance than a sack of potatoes. Its only value is in how fast it can be converted to cash.

In the mid-1950's a black market adoption scandal had broken in Montreal. A police investigation had discovered a group of lawyers who arranged private adoptions for babies born to unmarried girls. Large fees were charged the adoptive parents, so large in fact that it looked suspiciously as if the parents were buying the babies. The headlines were full of details about alleged baby brokering, falsified birth certificates, and the undercover work of the police officers who had made the case. One lawyer was convicted and subsequently disbarred. His law partner was acquitted.

Twenty years later, in 1975, an adoption scandal was again in the headlines, this time thanks to an investigation by the Montreal *Gazette*. Ironically, some of the names involved would be familiar to older readers who remembered the earlier incidents. The abuses uncovered were, if anything, worse than those of the 1950's.

The new scandal began with a telephone call from a tipster, one whose past information had always proven reliable and who had helped me on so many investigations that we had become personal friends. The tipster suggested that a group of local abortion referral agencies that had lately sprung up in the city might be involved in arranging private—and pricy—adoptions for the children of some of their clients who had been unable to go through with an abortion.

The tipster, though long on suspicions, was short on details. A trip to the clip files was called for.

According to the 1954–55 stories, only lawyers had been involved in the adoption rackets. The presence of abortion referral agencies, if it should be proven, would be a new wrinkle. But it was also a logical one. Why should a commercial agency that profited from the misfortune of pregnant girls seeking abortions turn down the chance to profit when the young women involved *didn't* want abortions? The situation made enough sense to bear looking into.

The first step was to identify the agencies that might be involved, as well as their owners and the names of their key employees. The second was to develop some way of discovering whether they arranged adoptions and, if so, under what circumstances.

Most of the city's abortion agencies advertised regularly in the tabloid newspapers. Some even advertised in the *Gazette*. A list was drawn up and, with the help of the tipster, regular checks of the rubbish outside the agencies' doors on trash pickup days were begun.

Every article having to do with adoptions or mentioning the name of any of the persons known to be involved with the local agencies was rooted out of the clip files and carefully read. Information from other cities was sought. I had read a wire service version of an adoption scandal in Cleveland, Ohio, and called the Cleveland *Plain Dealer* for information. They sent copies of the articles in question, as did the New York *Daily News*, which had carried the stories by Lynn McTaggart mentioned in Chapter I.

The reporters in both Cleveland and New York had obtained their information by posing as either unwed mothers with babies to sell or prospective adoptive parents. In this guise, they personally contacted lawyers and others suspected of involvement in the racket. This method appeared to be the only one likely to yield results.

Obviously, however, a male reporter could not pose as an unwed mother, no matter how glib a talker he might be. Equally evident was the probability that, while a few blind phone calls might net some information, it would take a lot more than that to clinch the story.

Personal interviews in the presence of witnesses and a cover story that would withstand attempts by a suspect to check it out were required.

Not without difficulty, the paper was persuaded to install a direct telephone line, not routed through the newspaper's switchboard, in a special office. That way, if a suspect called back a number given in my initial contact, he or she would not be greeted by a cheery voice saying: "Good afternoon, this is the *Gazette!*"

To prevent other reporters from picking up the phone if it rang in my absence, a note was taped to the dial warning them off. A tape recorder and telephone jack were also attached to the receiver, after having first checked with the legal advisor of the Montreal Urban Community Police Department to be sure its use was permissible.

Valuable Precaution

Several young women who could play the part of unwed mothers were then lined up and coached on how to act. Two of them were reporters and a third was one of my regular tipsters, Theresa Kennedy. The young women could also do double duty as mock wives if an agency asked for an interview with both prospective adoptive parents. False names and backgrounds were invented to be used as covers, and applications in these names were filed with the city's legitimate adoption agencies, to put the reporters involved officially on record as seeking a child.

As it turned out, this latter precaution was valuable. An employee at one government adoption agency run by the social services department proved to be an inside contact for an abortion referral agency involved in the black market racket. That employee had access to the legitimate agency's files and would have warned the baby brokers away if our names had not been listed there.

The stage was set, the actors and actresses were in place, and it was time to begin playing the game of "Here I am, I'm a mark!"

Using a false name, I telephoned several abortion agencies and, in a suitably embarrassed tone, started making inquiries. I was a well-to-do business executive, recently transferred from Toronto to Montreal, and ordinarily wouldn't call an abortion agency for anything, I told them.

But my wife and I were desperate. No, we didn't want an abortion. Quite the opposite. We wanted a baby, but due to the shortage of infants available for adoption through regular government agencies there were no babies to be found. (This cover story reflected reality. In the mid-1970's there was a drastic shortage of infants available for adoption, partly because of the increased number of abortions and partly because of a recent trend among single mothers to keep their babies and raise them alone. Many childless couples who wanted to share their homes and lives with a child were truly desperate.) I told the agencies that a friend (meaning the tipster) had suggested we check with the abortion agencies on the slim chance that they might have run across cases of girls who were willing to adopt instead of abort.

Having already contacted the legitimate government agencies and been told there was a waiting list, we were confident our story would ring true. We were even able to drop the names of various local adoption officials with whom we'd spoken and to say, truthfully, that our names were on file with the department of social services.

The first couple of abortion agencies called came up negative. No, they said, none of their girls wanted to adopt. No, they had no idea where a couple could go to find a child.

But the third call struck paydirt. The woman who answered the telephone at the agency—call it Agency X—listened to the inquiry and said: "We [the agency] have another service where a girl who is too far gone in her pregnancy . . . the babies are adopted in New York State. It's the State of New York that pays for their expenses during pregnancy and everything as long as the baby is adopted over there."

This latter information was false. The state did not pay for such expenses. The parents would have to pay. Claiming that the state paid was just part of the agency's pitch to make its arrangements sound legitimate.

The abortion agency, it turned out, had recently begun advertising its supplementary "service" in the papers. It was called "Pregnancy Help," and the phone number in the ads was an extension line in the agency office. We were on the right track. Asked whether a Canadian adoptive couple could "get in on the act," the woman replied: "Maybe we could do something about it." I left my name and the phone number of the special line to the *Gazette* office.

Lightning struck again at the fourth agency—Agency Y. Its director admitted that she had "a personal list a mile long" of couples seeking to adopt who had been unable to find children through the government agencies. This "personal list" she shared with a worker at the government social services adoption center, whom she named.

"Whenever we find girls who really don't want one [an abortion], I will contact the worker and these people will be notified and it'll be handled as a private adoption," she said.

The idea of a government employee keeping a personal list of adoptive names for a private, commercial abortion agency sounded a bit fishy. A subsequent check with the social services department revealed that all adoptions it handled were supposed to be on a strict first-come, first-served basis. There was supposed to be only one master list.

Not only would a separate, private list circumvent the normal process, giving those on it an unfair advantage over other couples waiting for a child, it would also violate the rules of confidentiality in the adoption process, which were established by law. Such an arrangement would be "terribly unethical," a government spokesman said.

The story was beginning to shape up. But it wasn't enough that at least two local abortion agencies were involved in adoptions and that one of them seemed to have put a government employee in a ticklish ethical situation. A thorough story would have to report how much the parents were paying in these transactions, whether they paid directly to the agencies or to a lawyer middleman, and exactly how widespread the operation was. It would also have to report whether any laws were being broken.

Copies of the legal statutes governing adoptions were available in the newspaper library, and we read them thoroughly. According to the law, it was illegal for any money to change hands during the adoption process except for the legal fee—usually in the neighborhood of $50— of the lawyer who drew up the necessary papers. Confidentiality was also an absolute requirement. To protect the reputation of the natural mother who was giving up her child and the peace of mind of the adoptive parents, no one outside the government agency was ever to know the names of anyone involved. Even the natural mother was not supposed to be told who the adoptive parents were.

Any evidence we could find that money was changing hands or that confidentiality was not being respected would be proof that the law was being broken.

Reading the Rubbish

By "reading the rubbish" at the abortion agencies, we had found the names and addresses of several doctors and lawyers with whom the agencies dealt. I decided to call them under another assumed name.

One call was to a New York City physician who took both abortion referral and cosmetic plastic surgery patients from the Montreal agencies. This call was a revelation. Contacted by one of our masquerading crew of "unwed mothers," the doctor was almost comically eager to arrange an adoption for her child in New York. He launched into a sales pitch so transparently greedy that it turned the reporters' stomachs.

He offered to let the natural mother stay in his "private clinic" until the baby was born and to fly her boyfriend down to New York with her. "Two can live as cheaply as one," he said, with a thick foreign accent. "Take both of you a ticket. I won't say [on the court record of expenses] you are coming from Montreal. I'll say you're coming from farther. How about Saskatchewan? So the fare will be practically double!"

He noted that there would be no trouble meeting such expenses, as some adoptive parents he knew about "pay up to $10,000 for a baby." In the course of the conversation he also gave a version of New York adoption laws that was almost totally fictitious.

Canadian babies
JUL 14 1975
channeled to U.S.

By THOMAS PAWLICK
of The Gazette

An international network of doctors and lawyers, using abortion referral agencies as sources, is channeling newborn Canadian babies to childless couples in the U.S. who sometimes pay thousands of dollars to adopt them, The Gazette learned.

At least two Montreal abortion referral agencies, the Centre Inter-Provincial at 1454 de la Montagne and the Centre Betty Farhood, with offices at 7200 Hutchison and 7164 St. Hubert, respectively, also attempted recently to arrange private adoptions in this city for reporters posing as unwed mothers or prospective adoptive parents.

Neither centre is licensed as an adoption agency.

Several New York abortion centres which take abortion referrals from Montreal also offered over the phone to arrange expenses-paid private adoption for persons posing as pregnant Montreal women. One doctor contacted through a New York centre which deals with abortion agencies here said adoptive parents in the U.S. could pay up to $10,000 for a baby.

According to Mrs. Isabel Williams of the adoption section of the government-licenced Catholic Family and Children's Services, a division of Ville Marie Social Service Centre here, there is currently a "drastic shortage of babies available for adoption."

She said the number of infants under three years old adopted in the province has dropped from 64.5 per cent of total legal adoptions in 1970-71 to 47.9 per cent in 1973-74.

Other adoption officials agreed there is a shortage of babies, caused by increased use of birth control methods, abortion and an increasing number of unwed mothers opting to keep their children.

"In short," another official said, "a market has been created."

The Centre Inter-Provincial, managed by Jean L'Arrivee, advertises its adoption branch in Montreal newspapers as "Grossesse Aide," a service to help women "continue pregnancy." (Another centre with a similar name, "Grossesse Secours," is not connected with L'Arrivee and sends all its clients to authorized government agencies.

A reporter posing as a prospective adoptive parent who called the Centre Inter-Provincial was told by Mrs. Claudette Portugais "we have another service where a girl who is too far gone in her pregnancy ... the babies are adopted in New York state.

"It's the state of New York that pays for their expense (in private adoptions) during their pregnancy and everything as long as the baby is adopted over there," she said. "Everything is done through lawyers and judges and notaries and things like that."

According to Joseph Reid, of the Child Welfare League of America Inc. in New York City, neither the state of New York nor the courts there "have funds to pay for such things as the expenses of the mother in a private adoption.

COULD DO SOMETHING

"A girl from out of state, if she were residing here and destitute, could go through the welfare agency, which would help her financially, but in that case the adoption would be public and handled by an authorized social agency."

The Child Welfare League of America is a private, non-profit organization that sets stan-

---

News that newborn babies were being channeled from Canada to adoptive couples in the U.S. by a network of doctors, lawyers, and abortion referral agencies caused a nationwide sensation in Canada.

We now had a $10,000 figure and a greedy doctor willing to falsify court records to get a piece of it. But we had more than that.

A check of New York state and city authorities revealed that the doctor's abortion clinic had been ordered closed by the courts when an inspection of the premises showed it was in violation of health laws. Among the long string of violations was the fact that the operating room was "soiled and stained" with blood and full of houseflies.

The doctor, who also had a record of convictions for fraud and income tax evasion, was in the process of having his license to practice revoked. And this was the character to whom the Montreal agencies were sending young women patients! "He's quite a character, actually," said one New York health worker. "He dates a beauty queen and drives around in a white Cadillac convertible with white rabbit fur seat covers." Evidently, the business he did was profitable.

It was time for the next step. I contacted a friend on the Montreal police force Sgt. David Adamo, and told him about the case. I wanted not only a story but also to break up the racket and put its perpetrators away. So did the policeman, a dedicated officer who had made an earlier reputation as an expert on the gambling operations of the city's Mafia.

I gave him typed copies of our telephone conversations, transcribed from our tapes, and copies of all our notes. He gave me $1,000—in counterfeit bills—and a "body bug" eavesdropping device to wear when the opportunity came to actually put down cash for a baby. We contacted the abortion agencies again—and again—indicating our eagerness to adopt. Then, with my harem of reporter "wives," I settled down to wait for a break.

It was weeks before it came, and then it was only a partial break. One reporter, posing as an unwed mother, had swung an interview with the director of Agency Y, the one with the personal list. The director, oozing concern, met the reporter in a local restaurant and put the little mother's fictitious name on her list. "I'll call you, dear, when I find a nice couple," she said.

The nice couple, as it turned out, were myself and the second woman reporter posing as my wife. The abortion agency director was unaware of the coincidence, but we had outfoxed ourselves. Obviously, the various steps of the adoption process could not take place because the reporter posing as an unwed mother was not really expecting, and before much more time elapsed this would become evident. Unless we got very lucky and the agency director asked for cash in advance, we'd never be able to clinch it.

Then the other abortion agency—Agency X—called back. My "wife" and I had by now had a personal interview with this agency's office manager, who now informed us that she "had a girl" for us. This time the girl in question was not one of our own reporters.

The agency's owner, who we later discovered was himself using a false name, gave us the name of a local lawyer, saying the lawyer would handle things for us. We called the attorney, who told us the agency had filled him in on the case and added: "I can fix it up for you." We were ecstatic.

Up to this point, however, no fees had been quoted and no money had changed hands. Only the doctor in New York, who was speaking only for himself in the earlier call, had mentioned money. To make a case for the police, cash had to change hands.

We had to be careful, moreover, to avoid being guilty of entrapment, of actually asking the abortion agencies or lawyer to do things, or of offering them money. In all conversations, we had to talk around the subject, letting *them* make the offers and quote the prices. It was a difficult problem in diplomacy.

Once, the director of Agency Y phoned and asked for an immediate interview. We thought it was the Big Break. Wearing the policeman's loaned "bug" and carrying his counterfeit bills in my wallet, I went to the agency. Outside two detectives sat waiting in a parked car while the spools of their tape recorder turned. If a demand for money was made during the conversation, I was to hand over the marked counterfeit bills immediately, whereupon the police would come storming in and make an arrest.

As it happened, the agency director only wanted to tell me about the sweet young thing she'd found—meaning our own reporter again—who might give us her baby. As if this was not disappointment enough, the body bug conked out during the interview, and the policemen outside, hearing nothing over the microphone, got nervous. As I was leaving the agency I almost stumbled into one of them, waiting in the hallway outside, gun drawn and ready to break down the door. "I thought they'd spotted the bug," he said. "There was nothing coming over the mike, and I had visions of them kicking the hell out of you."

The false alarm was disappointing, but at least during the interview we had gotten the name of another lawyer. Agency Y's adoptions were handled by the partner of one of the two lawyers charged in the 1950's adoption scandal described earlier. The law firm was still up to its old tricks.

Finally, Agency X came through. Its office manager called to say that the girl they "had" was willing to give up her child when it was born, and the birth wasn't far off. They were sending the girl down to New York, where a doctor would hurry the process by inducing the birth prematurely. This, they thought, would please us because it would bring the day of adoption that much closer. Their theory, apparently, was to keep the paying customer happy. The possibility that the baby might suffer physical harm by being brought into the world prematurely seemed not to trouble them. But it troubled us.

We became even more agitated when the office manager told us the name of the New York doctor who would do the inducing. It was the same greedy fellow with the houseflies in his operating room. "He does everything for us, all our abortions, everything," the office manager explained. We were appalled.

It was good news as far as the story was concerned, but we were skewered on the horns of a moral dilemma. Should we allow an innocent girl to be treated by a virtual butcher and her baby to be endangered by premature birth? The answer was no. No story was .worth that. We would have to call a halt to the whole thing soon, even before money had changed hands and even if the proof we wanted so badly had not yet materialized.

Our last hope of salvaging the story in time was Mr. Fixit, the lawyer. If he quoted us a price or asked for money before the girl left for New York, we could still clinch the story and warn the girl in time.

The agency, unethically, had given us the natural mother's name, and thus we were confident that we would be able to reach her.

I telephoned the lawyer and told him I had suddenly been ordered to make a business trip to Europe that would take several weeks. My wife was nervous and afraid something would go wrong in my absence, I said. Could we talk to him before I left, to get enough details to permit her to handle the adoption in my absence? Hopefully, the "details" in question would include the price, to which I would have to agree before leaving. The lawyer took the bait. The next morning we were in his office.

But once again, fate intervened. Unknown to us, the lawyer's father picked that night to die. When the "husband and wife" reporter team walked into the attorney's office they were greeted by his partner, who told them the lawyer was "at the hospital," where we would have to telephone him. We wondered what the lawyer was doing at the hospital. Visions of an injured pregnant girl flashed through our minds. But the lawyer was only there making arrangements for his father's burial.

On the telephone, we asked the lawyer how to proceed and when the check for his fee would be due. He told us he would pick up the child at the hospital himself and deliver it to us. He said his fee would be "$500 for now; if there are any more expenses it can be handled later." At last, the lawyer had asked us for a down payment and quoted us a price.

With relief, we realized it was time to come out in the open. Money hadn't actually changed hands, which meant the police couldn't make an arrest, but we were willing to stop where we were rather than endanger the unwed mother and her child. All that was still needed to make a story were our suspects' excuses and denials.

These were almost humorous, in a tragic sort of way. We dialed each number in turn, the reels on our tape recorder turning. "You mean *you've* been conning *me!*" the director of Agency Y exclaimed, incredulous at the turn of events. A wily old con woman, she was used to the situation being the exact reverse. The owner of Agency X, whose real name we had by now discovered, pleaded: "You don't know the good we do for these girls!"

Under his real name, this particular fellow had a long police record. Before opening his agency and getting into the abortion and adoption business, he had been convicted on gambling charges and of selling obscene material. He had also been linked to, though not charged in connection with, a scheme to fix bets on hockey games at the Montreal Forum by having the game timer stop the clock at crucial times.

The owners of Agency Y apparently had many friends in the city who were concerned that a newspaper story could damage their reputation. As the article was being written, anonymous telephone calls kept coming in to the office, suggesting that the reporter would experience divers unpleasantnesses if anything was published. Other callers said nothing, but only breathed heavily into the receiver.

The story ran on July 14, 1975, on page one. The wire services picked it up and by July 15 nearly every paper in Canada was running it.

In the story, we were able to report that at least two local abortion referral agencies were involved in handling private adoptions and that one had a regular, advertised service that was channeling Canadian babies to New York. We reported that Canadian babies adopted in the United States could carry a price tag as high as $10,000, and that an adoption in Montreal would have cost $500 or more, when the usual fee for a government-handled adoption was only $50.

We were also able to report that the owner of one agency had a long criminal record and that the owner of another had an arrangement with a social service worker that was "terribly unethical." One agency had broken confidentiality by giving us the natural mother's name, and the doctor it used was a butcher.

Neither the agencies, the lawyers, nor the doctors involved had bothered to screen their adoptive parents. A child adopted through them might have gone to anyone who was able to pay—to a drunk, to someone who was psychologically unstable, or to a reporter going under a false name.

We also reported that a number of other lawyers and doctors in New York, whom we had telephoned, had offered to arrange adoptions for Montreal women in which the cost to parents could go as high as $20,000.

Good and Bad

The results of the article were a mixture of good and bad.

On the good side, we had gathered enough information on the city's abortion agencies to do several follow-up articles on their nonadoption activities, which were a catalog of horrors. In addition, the Quebec provincial government reacted to the scandal by introducing a bill in the legislature to outlaw some of the abuses we had found.

On the bad side, the police had not been able to make an arrest, and the cutting of several paragraphs from the typewritten story for reasons of space resulted in our being forced a few days later to print a "clarification" notice, though not an actual retraction. The Montreal lawyer who had quoted us the $500 fee claimed that the reference to a "network" of lawyers and doctors in the U.S. and Canada was untrue. He wasn't a member of an international network, he insisted, but strictly a local boy. The network reference had pertained to the other lawyers and doctors we had mentioned, whose names and activities had been cut from the story in the composing room. We had to print a statement that the lawyer was not part of a network, which weakened the story's impact.

Finally, although a bill to outlaw some of the abuses we had found was introduced, the party in power lost the next provincial election to the separatist party of René Levesque, and the bill died in committee.

Today, the two abortion agencies, the New York doctor (now devoid of his license but apparently not hindered by the fact), and all the lawyers are still in business. If we had been willing to risk the safety of the unwed mother and her child, if the paper had had more space available, or if the election had gone differently—who knows? Maybe the racket would have been smashed.

Several months later I stumbled on the case of another young girl who had become pregnant and gone to a Montreal abortion agency to arrange for her child to be adopted. They sent her to New York, where a social worker found her later, penniless and crying and wandering the street with her newborn baby.

She had gone to New York "expenses paid," but the child was born black, like its father, and the white adoptive parents backed out of the deal. The New York doctor threw her out of his private clinic, threatening to sue her for his unpaid bills. The Montreal agency that had sent her down wouldn't even talk to her on the phone, and when she and her child finally arrived back in Montreal by bus, she didn't have enough change left to pay her busfare to her parents' house.

The doctor was our friend with the flies in his operating room, and the Montreal agency was Agency X. The girl, who was a psychological wreck by now, refused to bring a complaint or to testify.

The key element in this investigation turned out to be the stalking phase, which made heavy use of personal and telephone interviews. Its chief weakness, as far as the reporters had any control over it, was in the publishing phase. The copy should have been watched more closely in the composing room to prevent those crucial paragraphs from being cut.

Chapter VII

DEAD MAN'S RESCUE

African dictator "Big Daddy" Field Marshal Dr. Idi Amin Dada, V.C., D.S.O., M.C., and Life President of Uganda, had been conducting a Cannibal King horror show of mayhem and murder for more than six years when the spreading ripples of his repressive rule finally made themselves felt one summer morning in 1977 in the suburbs of Montreal, 7,875 miles away.

It was the African tyrant's policies that ultimately sparked a long-distance manhunt, a missing persons story that began with a housewife and a reporter but eventually involved the Prime Minister of Canada, the U.S. Congress, the Central Intelligence Agency, and the most bizarre collection of other actors imaginable.

The seeds of the story had been planted earlier in the year, when a 55-year-old British tea expert, Mark Elias, decided that prospects for business success in Uganda outweighed the dangers posed by the unpredictable wrath of the impoverished country's leader.

Despite earlier warnings from the British government that subjects of Her Majesty Queen Elizabeth II would be well advised to stay out of Uganda, Elias went into the country. An old Africa hand whose knowledge of tea cultivation had earned him a reputation as the best tea man in East Africa, he planned to set up an agricultural engineering firm to supply the nation's coffee and tea plantations with machinery and expert consulting advice.

According to his daughter, he had been told by officials of the World Bank and the European Common Market that the situation had calmed down considerably in Uganda since the January murder of Anglican Archbishop Janan Luwuum, and that the risks to enterprise there were not as bad as newspaper headlines of the time made them out.

Elias might have gone into the country even without such assurances. A World War II British Army veteran described by his family as "incorrigibly adventurous," he had survived everything from malaria to volcanic eruptions during his career as a tea consultant in Indonesia and Africa.

"He'd been in Uganda before and knew the people there well," said his daughter, a dark-haired, quiet-voiced woman of twenty-five who was working as a substitute teacher at a high school in Montreal. "He'd been working as a tea estate manager and consultant on and off for the past thirty years, and he went to Uganda first in 1965 at the government's invitation to help set up a model tea plantation. He worked in neighboring Rwanda for a couple of years afterward on a similar project and was thinking of retiring.

"But then a friend came up with the engineering firm proposition and he changed his mind. He said if he retired he was afraid sitting around doing nothing would kill him. He was always totally unaware of politics and a bit naive. He once said he wondered if he didn't have a charmed life."

If he did, the charm ceased working in May 1977, shortly after President Amin was told that his presence would not be welcome at the international British Commonwealth Conference in London. Carrying a British passport in Uganda at such a time may well have put Elias in the path of a storm. Amin did not take kindly to diplomatic snubs and when offended had a way of lashing out at whatever—or whoever—was nearby.

Elias apparently sensed that something was coming before the storm struck. "We had a telephone call from Dad early in May," recalled his daughter. "You could tell it was being tapped. There was a two-second delay between our questions and his answers and you could hear clicks. The Ugandans weren't very good at tapping phones.

"He was cheerful and kept saying 'everything's fine,' but I wasn't reassured at all. He didn't sound himself. About two weeks later we got a birthday letter from him for my son, who was two. It was a strange letter, rambling and almost incoherent. I began to get worried then." The birthday letter was the last word his family ever heard from Mark Elias.

A Sob Story

My own involvement in the case began when the city editor of the Montreal *Gazette* called me over to his desk one morning and said that one of the paper's receptionists had a relative "in the slammer" in Uganda. "It sounds like a good sob story," he explained. "Go on out and talk to them. You know, the tearful family and all that."

Elias was probably dead, I was told, but this was a chance to get one up on the Toronto *Star*. The *Gazette* had recently reprinted a long series of articles by the *Star's* Gerald Utting, recounting his experiences in Amin's Makindye Jail. Here was an opportunity for the paper to get an Amin story of its own, however brief.

A *Gazette* receptionist was actually a relative by marriage of Elias' "tearful family," which turned out to include the missing man's two daughters, his second wife, his son-in-law, and two grandchildren. Sitting in the kitchen of the eldest daughter's suburban home, they were brave and determined, rather than tearful, and had taken a calculated risk in allowing the receptionist to alert the paper to their plight.

Elias' 35-year-old wife, Susan, who had recently flown to Montreal from her home in London, England, recounted the tale. While Elias' daughter was worrying over his letter and strange phone call, his wife was also upset. Her worry turned to outright fear on May 23, when a cryptic call came from the British Foreign Office. A slim blonde with a mind as quick as her feet are on a tennis court, Susan Elias was an intensely loyal woman, and her impatience with bunglers showed in her retelling of the call.

"I got this vague call from Whitehall," she said. "An old, bumbling idiot came on the line, stuttering with this Colonel Blimp accent, and asked: 'Is your husband Mark Elias? We can't seem to trace him. Mumble, mumble, wonder if he's the same fellow, y'know.' He said they were pursuing inquiries 'as it seems we don't know his whereabouts' and that he'd call back. Then he just rang off. The call came right out of the blue, and naturally it made me frantic.

"I telegraphed Nairobi immediately, to a friend of Mark's, asking him to confirm that everything was OK. On May 27 I got the friend on the phone and he told me he'd heard on May 18 that Mark was missing. He said the British High Commission in Nairobi had asked him not to tell me anything so as not to panic me.

"Not tell his wife! And then that cryptic call from Whitehall. By this time I was boiling and phoned the Foreign Office myself. I gave them Mark's description, his car license plate number and so forth, and asked what had happened to him. They said they didn't know anything and, as far as searching for him was concerned, weren't even sure he was missing. They said they'd call back if they heard anything. Don't call us, we'll call you.

"By now I was really worried, but I couldn't get a straight answer out of anybody. I called the former British High Commissioner for Uganda, but he couldn't get anything out of the Foreign Office either. Finally, I phoned my Member of Parliament, Michael Mates, and got some action. He phoned the Foreign Secretary and was told that Mark was definitely missing. The Foreign Office said they hadn't informed me because they were 'afraid of having a ranting, raving wife on their doorstep.'

"Finally, with Mates' help, I got a more sympathetic Foreign Office man, who began ringing me up regularly to say they'd heard nothing. He told me specifically not to involve the press, as it might aggravate the situation with Uganda. Then it just went on like that, for several weeks."

Across the Atlantic in Canada Elias' two daughters, and a son living in Vancouver, also waited for word, but none came. Unknown to them, the British government knew more than it was telling. As British Vice-Consul Peter Palmer later explained, what Whitehall knew was strictly speaking "only hearsay," but might have been enough to cause the family to despair.

Britain, which had broken diplomatic relations with Uganda, had no official representatives in that country and had to carry on any business with Amin's government via intermediaries from other nations. Two polite notes of inquiry from the British High Commission in Nairobi, Kenya, asking for news of Elias had drawn no response from the Ugandan capital. Nonofficial sources in Amin's territory, however, had managed to get word out that Elias had been arrested on May 13 by agents of the dreaded State Research Bureau, the band of armed Nubian thugs who terrorized the country, murdering Amin's political enemies and reaping their reward in plunder from the homes and dead bodies of their victims.

The British also knew that on the night of May 13 a white man's body, riddled with bullets, had been seen lying on the Masaka Road, about eight kilometers outside Kampala on the route to Rwanda. Only Elias, Canadian journalist Gerald Utting, and Robert Scanlon, an Englishman who had taken Ugandan citizenship, were known to be in trouble in Uganda. Both Utting and Scanlon were seen alive in prisons, and Utting, author of the Toronto *Star's* series, was shortly released. Only Elias was unaccounted for.

The conclusion was obvious, but no one was about to draw it for Elias' family. They were told nothing about the body. Instead, they were left to worry and, eventually, to launch an eight-month fight to release a man who they thought was in prison but was already dead.

It was a brave fight. In Montreal, Elias' eldest daughter began writing letters and working the telephone. With two young children to care for and a teaching job to hold down she didn't have much time, but she used every spare minute.

She contacted the British consulate in Montreal, the Ugandan High Commissioner's office in Ottawa, and her own Canadian federal government. No one knew anything. The Canadian government told her they had no jurisdiction because Elias was not a Canadian citizen. Even if they had jurisdiction, they preferred to wait until journalist Utting was free before taking any action on another case. When in due course Utting was freed, the Canadian government said it would only relay information to Elias' family from the British. The British said they knew nothing.

She wrote the United Nations Human Rights Commission, but was told nothing could be done until a UN mission visited Uganda several months later, and that even this mission could only report on human rights violations in general, not on individual cases.

Harvest of Rumors

In England Susan Elias was also busy. She badgered the Foreign Office and MP Mates. She contacted Gloria Scanlon, the wife of the other Englishman in trouble in Uganda. She wrote or called most of Elias' business friends in Africa.

What the two women reaped for their efforts were rumors. One source told them that a man answering Elias' description had been seen in Makindye Military Prison in Kampala, thin and bearded but alive. Another source said Elias had been seen drinking with a mysterious white man named "Bob Paul" in the Cape Town Villas Hotel the night before his May 13 disappearance, but nobody knew who or where Bob Paul was, or how Elias met him. There was speculation that Bob Paul may actually have been Robert Astles, the British-born owner of the hotel and close confidant of Amin.

Elias' wife decided that if Bob Paul existed he might know what had happened to her husband. The British Foreign Office told her not to say anything about the affair in public, but she went ahead and placed an advertisement asking Bob Paul to contact her. The ad appeared in newspapers and was broadcast on radio in Liverpool, from which city Paul was rumored to have come. The only result of the ad was to irritate Whitehall, which didn't want publicity.

Meanwhile, stories of Amin's atrocities continued to fill the headlines. Reports of Christian tribesmen being massacred and of enemies of the regime being tortured and the publication of a book by former Ugandan cabinet minister Henry Kyemba took turns for media attention. Kyemba, living in exile, received considerable attention when he accused his former master of cannibalism. Amin, he said, ate the hearts of his victims.

By mid-July the family had had enough and decided to risk turning to the *Gazette* for help. After talking to Elias' family and learning more about Amin's unpredictable behavior, however, it seemed reckless to simply splash a hostile story on page one without reflecting on its possible consequences. It seemed wiser to tread cautiously. Perhaps a phone call or letter to the Ugandan High Commission in Ottawa, from a newspaper rather than an individual citizen, would get better results. The threat of bad publicity might prompt cooperation where a hostile story already in print might only bring retaliation on Elias. The family agreed that this made sense.

We decided to telephone the Ugandan High Commission in Ottawa, which functioned as the de facto embassy. The commissioner wasn't in, but his obviously fearful receptionist unwisely gave out his home phone number and his name, Modesto Ombiga. The man who answered the home number listened silently until Elias' name and that of the paper were mentioned, then protested in a shaking voice: "You have the wrong number! This is not the Ugandan government," and hung up.

Rumor had it that Ugandans abroad were watched by Amin's agents. Most had relatives still at home and feared for their safety. Getting involved in delicate matters was dangerous, and Elias' case looked delicate. Repeated calls to the High Commission, however, brought a request to put the inquiry in writing and "we will look into it." A registered letter on newspaper letterhead was duly sent.

The *Gazette* editors were impatient at the delay, demanding to know why a story couldn't run immediately. I asked an External Affairs Department official in Ottawa what that might do. "It might get him killed," the official said. The editors grudgingly agreed to wait, and on July 28 a letter came to the paper from a Lamech E. Akong'o, Ugandan High Commissioner in Ottawa (Ombiga had been shifted). It said: "I have informed authorities in Kampala of the anxiety of the relations of Mr. Elias and asked them to do what they can to remove the cause of their anxiety."

The wording of the note—"to remove the cause"—was not exactly reassuring, but it was the first written response from a Ugandan official since Elias had been missing. It was also the last communication the family was to get from Amin's government.

Days, then weeks, dragged by with no word. I suggested another route. I called Ottawa and asked if the Canadian government could not request information from Kampala, since Elias' family at least were Canadian citizens. Elias' daughter had already tried to get Ottawa to do this, but now a newspaper was asking.

Eventually I was put in contact with Ivan Head, Prime Minister Pierre Trudeau's personal foreign policy advisor and a federal government Big Gun. Could not Trudeau make a personal, informal appeal to Kampala for information, I asked? It was obvious to Head that this question, between the lines, carried a threat. How would it look, after all, for Trudeau to be reported in the press as having refused to make a humanitarian gesture on behalf of a Canadian family?

Head seized the implication immediately: "Anything that affects Canadians affects the government," he said. "Yes, the Prime Minister's office would be willing to do it." He asked, however, that Trudeau's intervention not be publicized.

Elias' daughter, cynical after weeks of official brush-offs, doubted that such a request would actually be made. Both she and the reporter doubted that it would be pressed with much energy as long as it remained a private matter. Accordingly, Head's office was called back again, this time to tell him the family was going ahead with a story in the paper. Head wasn't in. The government's official public relations department was phoned and told of the impending story, and they promised to relay the message to Head "right away."

The first story ran on August 26, 1977, on page one.

"Prime Minister Pierre Trudeau has joined a Montreal family in their efforts to contact their father, who was reported missing in Uganda in May and has since been located in Kampala's Makindye Prison," the article said, basing the prison reference on what later proved to be an erroneous report from Africa.

The paper's editors had wanted to spice up the story with gory references to conditions in Makindye and to Amin's ferocity. An angry protest by the reporter succeeded in keeping the references out. There was no reason yet to risk Amin's anger and put Elias in danger, especially not for the sake of mere "color" in the story.

The married name of Elias' daughter and her home address were also left out, thus making it impossible for other papers to contact her. This was to be a *Gazette* exclusive, a thumb of the nose at Toronto, and that is how it worked out. "I've been getting calls all morning," the jubilant city editor said the next day. "One guy even offered to pay me if I'd give him the family's phone number. The Toronto *Star* is going nuts!"

The article put the Prime Minister's office publicly on record as promising to help Elias' family. To refuse to press the matter, now that voter/readers were aware of it, would obviously be bad public relations for Trudeau. Head, knowing the government had been boxed in, was furious. "I've been used," he snapped over the phone.

"If we hadn't used him, would Trudeau have done anything about my father?" Elias' daughter snapped back.

Whether the Prime Minister would have helped or not turned out to be of little consequence. The Ugandans ignored Pierre Trudeau, just as they were by this time ignoring Elias' wife and daughter. Canada's request for information was never answered.

A Surreal Night

The Ugandan government even had trouble answering telephones. On August 22, frustrated at the lack of results, Elias' wife (who had flown to Montreal from England), his eldest daughter, and the *Gazette* reporter decided to try telephoning Amin himself, via transatlantic hookup, in hopes of making a personal appeal to his humanity. It was an all-night effort and took on a weird air of surrealism before it was over.

The offer by Pierre Trudeau, Prime Minister of Canada, to intercede on behalf of a prisoner in Idi Amin's infamous Makindye Prison was carried on Page 1 of the Montreal Gazette.

Elias' daughter had somehow obtained the number of the State Command Post in Kampala, which was supposedly official Ugandan government headquarters, so there seemed at least a slim possibility that we might be able to get through to the president.

Unfortunately the family had been preceded by a small army of newsmen and pranksters who had been calling Kampala regularly from overseas ever since Amin's antics had begun making headlines. Every nut in Europe or America, it seemed, wanted to talk to "Big Daddy" Amin.

The Canadian overseas operator chuckled knowingly when told the call was to Kampala. "Don't tell me," she said. "You want to talk to President Amin Dada, right?"

"How did you guess?"

"Everybody wants to talk to him. Besides, I think he's about the only one over there who has a line."

It was midnight in Montreal, 8 A.M. across the world in Kampala. The call was placed person-to-person, to save money in case Amin was unreachable. A man with a squeaky, high-pitched voice and a sing-song African accent answered the phone.

"State Command Post!"

"Hello, this is Montreal calling. I want to speak to President Idi Amin."

"This is he," said the squeaky voice. There was a pause. It seemed incredible.

"*You* are President Amin?"

Another pause, then, with embarrassment: "Well, no. Not really. I *wish* I was. This isn't where he is. This is just an office with a name." To contact Amin, the squeaky voice said, "you have to call his Principal Private Secretary for an appointment." We took the secretary's number and dialed it. The secretary wasn't in.

"He's just phoned, though, to say he's on his way in to the office," said the receptionist. "He should be here in five or ten minutes."

When told the reason for the call, however, the receptionist's tone changed from one of cheerful goodwill to obvious fear. His voice trembled. "He [the Principal Private Secretary] won't be in today," he said suddenly. "The secretary just called to say he won't be in for a week, I think."

"But you just said . . ."

"There's nobody here. Nobody will be here for a week!"

"But *you're* there . . ."

The voice was flustered. "No, I'm not. Nobody's here!" He hung up. We dialed again, and again, through a succession of overseas operators. At last someone in the secretariat decided to risk talking. He gave a phone number in Entebbe, that of the secretary at Amin's personal residence.

The Bell Canada operator wanted to know to whom she should bill the call. "Is this the Principal Private Secretary, Mr. Akochu?" she asked.

"Akok-who?"

"Is this the party I'm calling? I must know to make the bill."

"There is no Bill here."

"No, no. This is a call from Canada to Mr. Akochu. If he is speaking I can bill him."

"You want to bill him for what?"

"For this call! Is he there?"

"Who?"

"Ohhhh!" groaned the operator. "What are these people? It's like talking to the moon!" The Ugandan hung up.

By now, the little group around the kitchen table in Elias' daughter's house had been on the telephone for two hours and were starting to get giddy. A whiskey bottle was broken out, and with each new absurdity they couldn't help laughing. Elias' life was at stake, they believed, but they couldn't help it. Whiskey and nerves.

At the Entebbe number another man answered. It was 10 A.M. there, 2 A.M. in Montreal. "To talk to our president you must go through the Principal Private Secretary or the Minister of Information," the man said.

"Who is the minister? What is his name?"

"I don't know."

"You are on the president's staff and you don't know the minister's name?"

"I can tell you who it was last week. There have been several. But he is new in his post, I think."

And so it went. Four hours, five. At last, tipsy and exhausted, the group made its last effort. A woman, humming to herself, answered. "No talk now!" she said. "I'm doing my hair!" We insisted, saying we were calling about Mark Elias. A man came on the line and asked how to spell Elias.

"E, as in Edward; L, as in Lassie . . ."

"Who is that?"

"Lassie is a dog. I, as in ignorant . . ."

The man hung up. Perhaps he had gotten the intended message. We tried the same number again and got a telephone operator in neighboring Kenya, then the Uganda operator. "State House has instructed they will take no more calls today," the latter said, and rang off.

"This is very unusual," said the operator in Nairobi. "All the circuits to Uganda seem to be cut off. There are no phone lines open in the country!"

"You mean they've cut off everyone's phone in the whole country just to get rid of us?"

"They must have. Maybe there is a breakdown somewhere."

The little group gave it up. It was 7 A.M. Montreal time. The crank callers to Uganda had done their job. The call by Elias' family was probably never taken seriously.

Over the next few weeks they contacted the Soviet Consulate in Montreal, hoping that the Russians, with their military advisors in Uganda, would have more influence with Amin than did Canada. It was a bizarre but wasted effort.

Elias' daughter took a day off from teaching and went by cab with me to the rambling old mansion on the slopes of Mount Royal where the consulate was housed. Lenin's portrait frowned grimly down from the wall as we waited in an anteroom, clutching a laboriously composed letter for the consul. It quoted Soviet poet Yevgeny Yevtushenko and begged the consul to show that he, like the poet, was "a member of the nation of men of good will," by helping Elias' family.

The vice-consul who interviewed us was not a poetry fan. All we got for the effort was the realization that our words had probably been taken down for posterity on some Royal Canadian Mounted Police tape recorder, bugging the Russian consulate.

The missing man's daughter got a somewhat more sympathetic hearing in Ottawa, where Canadian Member of Parliament Dr. Morris Foster arranged an interview with a visiting Kenyan MP who had contacts in Uganda. The Kenyan was interested and spoke frankly. "He [Amin] is a madman. There are many Ugandans who flee to Kenya. I know some people in Uganda, like General Umbolo. He is crazy too, but is a sort of strongman. I will not involve my government. It will be private. But I will try to find your father for you."

The Kenyan's long, thin fingers twitched nervously as he played with a cigarette. It was obvious that he was sticking his neck out, and it was agreed not to mention his name publicly. He did try to find Elias, but like everyone else he failed.

So did Joshua Nkomo, the Rhodesian black guerrilla leader who was then embroiled in the struggle to end Ian Smith's white minority regime. Elias' daughter and I met Nkomo in Montreal, where he had come on a speaking tour seeking support for his battle to change Rhodesia from a white supremacist enclave to a new, black-ruled nation called Zimbabwe. Amin had publicly praised Nkomo's guerrillas and might listen to such a leader, we theorized.

A huge man with graying hair and a stern face, Nkomo was an imposing figure. He moved and spoke slowly, with gravity, and his eyes reflected a life of suffering. He had himself been imprisoned for many years by the Smith regime, and he smiled gently at Elias' daughter. "It is very hard to be separated from your family, I know," he said. "I've read about your father's case, but until now he was only a name. Now there is a face and a family connected with that name. I will do my best to try to help you."

The editors of the *Gazette,* meanwhile, had tired of the story. When it was suggested that the paper might pay for Elias' flight home, should he eventually be released, or for his wife to fly to Nairobi to meet him, the idea was rejected.

The editors were reminded that Elias was a relative of a *Gazette* employee and that if he were freed it would be in large part due to the paper's help. It would make a great story to be able to arrange for the family's reunion, along with exclusive interviews with "the man the *Gazette* rescued from Amin." Neither Elias' wife, who had already spent a good deal of money, nor his daughter could easily afford a flight to Africa, whereas the plane fare wouldn't be much more than what the paper had paid for the right to reprint the Utting articles mentioned earlier.

"We've already had the story as far as I'm concerned," said the managing editor. Asking for help with the plane fare on grounds that it might net an exclusive interview was "just a sophisticated form of blackmail," he said. "I can't believe he wouldn't talk [to other papers]. I can't believe you [the reporter] or them [the family]." Time to work on the case was subsequently curtailed, and new assignments were issued by the city desk. From then on, any work on the Elias story was on my own time.

The missing man's daughter began losing hope and his wife grew more and more depressed. Tears came frequently. Mrs. Elias finally left Montreal for Vancouver, to stay with Elias' son by a former marriage. "She was afraid she'd crack if she stayed any longer," said the daughter.

It was mid-October and still no news of Elias. Six months. Bureaucrats in Ottawa and England no longer bothered to call. The family had to write or phone them for news, often calling long distance and always at their own expense. But Elias' daughter kept trying.

The fate of Robert Scanlon, Amin's other British victim, was reported in the papers. "British-born businessman Robert Scanlon, detained in Uganda four months ago on charges of spying for Britain, was beaten to death with a sledgehammer in a Kampala prison September 14, according to an eyewitness," the story said.

"Oh God," winced Elias' daughter, reading the account. She redoubled her efforts. At my suggestion the president of the Quebec Islamic Center in Montreal was contacted. Amin and his Nubian killers were

Muslims. Perhaps a plea from that quarter would be recognized. The mosque president, Izhar A. Mirza, at first was doubtful but finally agreed to write Amin, appealing in the name of Allah for mercy for Elias. The letter received no response.

Trade Boycott

Reports had appeared in the papers earlier that U.S. Representative Donald Pease of Ohio had sponsored a bill in the House of Representatives calling for an American trade boycott against Uganda because of Amin's human rights violations. Elias' daughter agreed that it might be worthwhile to contact Pease.

She also suggested pleading with the American Tea Growers Association, many of whose member firms had dealt with her father in the past. "He's done a lot of work for them," she said. "Some of the people there got their start in business because of Dad. He's done favors for a lot of them."

Representative Pease and his assistant, William Gould, were eager to help, but the rest of official Washington wasn't. Unlike Pease, who could use the Elias case as an example in drumming up support for his bill, no one else had anything to gain by involving themselves.

Pease and Gould might have helped Elias' family even without the boost it could give their bill. Both seemed genuinely concerned. The Congressman's office contacted the U.S. State Department, and, because one rumor had circulated that Elias might have been accused of spying, also contacted the U.S. Central Intelligence Agency (CIA).

On October 24 Gould called with a progress report. He had discovered that the then Ugandan chargé d'affaires in Washington was himself suspected of spying and that the U.S. government was looking for a pretext to expel him. If Elias' daughter wrote the chargé asking for information on her father and he refused to give it, Gould said, "it could be used as further evidence here that he should be expelled."

Elias' daughter telephoned the Ugandan chargé on October 27, and was refused an answer. "He wouldn't even give me his name over the phone," she said. On October 28 Gould said that the State Department had apparently decided not to move after all. "It may be weeks or not till next year before they decide what to do," he added.

Hope for action by the State Department diminished further on November 9. A group of Ugandans had been discovered by the press in Texas, taking flying instructions in an apparent deal with a helicopter firm. The news that the Carter administration, while publicly expressing support for human rights, had allowed Amin's men to come to the U.S. for technical training caused a flap.

"State is very uptight about this Texas thing," said Gould. "They're superdefensive about anything to do with Uganda and suggest it would be best to hold off." As for the spying rumor against Elias, he added: "We've had a briefing with the CIA and they said he was not affiliated with them." (Elias, another source had told his daughter, had friends in the U.S. consulate in Rwanda and had phoned them several times from Uganda, which may have made Amin's State Research Bureau thugs suspicious.)

As for the American Tea Growers Association, a contact there who knew Elias was trying to persuade members to send Amin a note requesting information. But the association moved slowly. Despite constant badgering by Elias' daughter, the final draft of a letter wasn't typed until October 23. It had to wait for signature until several members off at conventions returned to their offices. The association's note, sent months after it had been asked for, received no reply.

The Elias family was running out of options. "Dad had so many friends," mused his daughter. "It's unreal that nobody can do anything, that everyone's efforts are ignored." Elias' wife, depressed and angry, snapped: "All the British government does is sit on their backsides counting telexes while Mark waits in jail!"

The weeks wore on, and it was January 1978. The phone rang at my home one evening. By now I had changed jobs. The call was from Elias' daughter, and her voice on the phone had a strange, flat quality to it. Sounding as if she were speaking in a trance, she said: "The British vice-consul was here today. Dad's dead."

There was a pause, as if she were collecting herself. Then she continued: "It was Peter Palmer. He said the British government had 'been informed that reliable sources in Uganda have concluded your father is dead. You can take this as absolute confirmation.'" A description of Elias' last day had been pieced together from various government reports and sources in Africa, she said.

"Dad apparently left the Cape Town Villas Hotel the morning of May 13 and went to the Rwandan embassy in Kampala to get a visa to travel to Rwanda by car. He'd also booked a flight to Rwanda for the following Wednesday, which indicates he must have felt threatened. He went back to his office to write a few letters and told the staff there he'd had a 'bloody awful morning.' One of the letters he wrote was to my son Timothy, that long rambling one. He left the office around noon and was never seen alive again. Later that day Ugandan Army jeeps surrounded the hotel.

"That night a Ugandan official, who disappeared himself in September, reported that the body of a white man had been seen on the Masaka Road. Apparently my father had tried to escape in his car, but State

Research Bureau thugs followed him. When they got to a deserted stretch of road where there were no lights, they ambushed and shot him, leaving his body in the road.

"I can almost feel how he must have felt, alone on a dark road and suddenly feeling bullets ripping into your body. It's disgusting. He was there creating jobs, this is how they thank him!" The dead man's wife, she said, was too upset to talk. "She just broke down when she heard. She said she was going to just go for a long walk in the woods out there in British Columbia."

The long fight was over.

According to Palmer, the family had not been informed earlier about the body in the Masaka Road because "it was purely a rumor that the body was Elias." The British had been informed of Elias' disappearance and the sighting of the body as early as May 14. Elias' wife was not told he was missing until nine days later, the day of the cryptic call from the "bumbling idiot" at Whitehall.

Elias' family had spent eight nerve-wracking months fighting to rescue a dead man.

Why was Elias killed? Nobody can say for certain. It may have been because he was British at a time when Amin was angry at the British Commonwealth's diplomatic snub. It may have been the phone calls from Uganda to the U.S. embassy in Rwanda, making Amin's thugs suspicious of spying. Perhaps, as Elias' wife once wondered, it was because the mysterious "Bob Paul" saw Elias as a business rival and decided that a spying accusation would get rid of the competition.

The Ugandan government never gave a reason. In fact, it never officially admitted even that it knew Elias was dead. It was a bizarre government, living a real-life horror show.

"I've been to Uganda," said the victim's daughter. "It used to be a beautiful country and the people there are good, friendly people. But after Amin took over it turned into a pigsty. You could see the difference at the Kenya/Uganda border. On the Kenyan side, the asphalt road is new and fresh, with a neat white centerline. On the Ugandan side the potholes start immediately.

"There are old, rusting junk cars left lying along the road: no gasoline and nobody who knows how to drive them. Kenyan farms are irrigated and the bush is lush green. Uganda, by comparison, is a desert.

"But I've done my crying. I have no tears left. Amin butchered thousands, and the U.S. and England continued to trade with him, buying his coffee and supplying the currency he needed to keep his band of thugs happy. They propped him up and then went and cried about human rights. It's hypocritical."

When a regime is a source of profits, even small profits, it's easier to regard a massacre or two as a joke. Idi Amin Dada was easy to laugh at, with his grandiose speeches and titles, his many wives and his unpredictable temper. Perhaps the West, with its undercurrent of racism, somehow needed the reinforcement of prejudices Amin gave it. The image of Queen Elizabeth II, full of Windsor dignity, smiling up from a British postage stamp while the barbaric cannibal king looks down at the letter with envy was, after all, a reassuring image.

When Amin finally fell, chased out of Uganda by black troops from Tanzania, not a few white supremacists were disappointed.

As a missing persons story, a long-distance manhunt, the Elias story must be reckoned a failure. It failed to rescue the victim and disappointed the editors who had hoped to turn it into a splashy circus. In justice, however, success was beyond any of the actors' control right from the start. Elias was already dead and couldn't be brought back to life.

Those involved had done their best, through the original background-ing, planning, and stalking phases, and no possibility was left unexplored or unexploited.

Every book, newspaper, or magazine article on Uganda or Amin was sifted for information that could help find a lever to move the missing man's captors. The Elias children's own memories and knowl-edge of Africa were discussed and reexamined endlessly for possible leads. Ugandan officials in Ottawa and Kampala were approached cir-cumspectly, and our own published stories were carefully worded so as not to anger or frighten them. The pressure that was brought to bear came only after more polite efforts had failed.

Elias' death and the Ugandan government's refusal to speak made it impossible to clinch the story with the prisoner's release or to get the formal "malefactor's reply," but there was a follow-up. With the family's permission, I wrote the report of Elias' death for the Montreal *Star,* and in it his children at last said what they really felt, blasting both Amin and the British and Canadian governments, which had done so little, and with such reluctance, to help.

"I'd like to contact the group of Ugandan exiles in the U.S. who are trying to fight Amin," Elias' eldest daughter said. "I'd like to help Congressman Pease get his boycott bill passed, too, if he thinks it could help unseat Amin. I'd like to see Amin gone." She had not given up her fight, even though her father was beyond saving, and when the dictator at last fell, pursued across his ruined land by his own angry people as he fled to Libya, she must have felt satisfaction.

Elias' children, through the *Gazette* and Montreal *Star* stories, had proven their solidarity with their father and with all of Amin's victims. From that standpoint, at least, the dead man's rescue was a success.

Chapter VIII

THE SILENT TOLL

The publicity surrounding the near-meltdown at the Three Mile Island nuclear power plant near Harrisburg, Pennsylvania, on March 28, 1979, was almost as great as that which accompanied the Kennedy assassination in 1963. Ask anyone who was within earshot of a radio or television at the time, and chances are they still remember precisely where they were and what they were doing "when the reactor went haywire." Millions of printed pages and hundreds of broadcast hours were devoted to the subject for months after the accident.

A year afterward, however, the events at Three Mile Island seemed to have been "covered to death," examined, reexamined, and nitpicked in such detail as to become downright boring to public and newsmen alike. "No one died at Three Mile Island," the utilities and government spokesmen insisted, and, with the cleanup of the mess inside the stricken reactor well under way, the event looked to most reporters like ancient history.

Unfortunately for those affected, the story wasn't over. In fact, the real tale of the disaster at TMI had not yet been told.

The editors of *Harrowsmith Magazine* got their first hint that the true facts had not been made public when a reader in Afton, Virginia—provoked by an earlier letter to the editor that had repeated the "no one died at Three Mile Island" refrain—decided to write a letter to the editor of her own. "What about all the babies that have been born in the Harrisburg area with malformed thyroid glands or who died shortly after birth?" asked subscriber Wendy Watson.

The statement was startling. None of the numerous reports on the accident had mentioned anything about dead or injured babies. Was Ms. Watson a crackpot, or did she know something no one else did?

The magazine's copy readers, who normally review letters to the editor for accuracy, grammar, and the possibility of libel, felt obligated to check this one further. Head copy editor Alice O'Connell made a telephone check of various environmental and energy lobbying groups to see if they had heard anything about dead babies in Harrisburg. None had. Then Ms. O'Connell recalled that a U.S. scientist, Dr. Ernest Sternglass of the University of Pittsburgh, had predicted fatal consequences from the accident. She decided to find him.

Reached in Bloomington, Indiana, Dr. Sternglass turned out to be unexpectedly voluble. Yes, he said, the radioactivity released during the TMI accident had indeed killed children, whose bodies are much more sensitive to radiation than are those of adults. Statistics readily available to the public proved it. All along the pathways followed by the drifting clouds of radioactive gases, from Harrisburg north through New York State and into Canada, infant mortality statistics had risen and would continue to rise. A minimum of 430 infant deaths could be ascribed to their exposure to radioactive gases from Three Mile Island.

"This is an incredible story," said Ms. O'Connell. "But why is no one reporting it?"

"Think about it," said Sternglass, his tone making his meaning obvious. The term "cover-up" went unspoken but was clearly implied.

The existence of a Watergate-style cover-up in connection with the accident seemed at least a logical possibility. It would, after all, be against the vested interests of both the government and the electric utility companies to allow it to be known that nuclear power was as dangerous as Sternglass was suggesting. The U.S. government is heavily committed to nuclear weapons for defense and to nuclear power as a means of ending the West's dependence on Arab oil. The utilities have invested millions of dollars in building nuclear power plants. Shutting the reactors down would deprive the military of a major source of nuclear weapons material and cost the utilities a fortune. The utilities also stood to lose additional millions in damage lawsuits from persons who might have been hurt by exposure to radioactivity.

As for the news media, which would normally be expected to report the effects of a nuclear accident, their own biases and limitations would also tend to prevent them from doing so. Most daily newspapers give very little depth coverage to science, and few but the largest papers have staff members capable of understanding the complexities of nuclear physics. Even papers that employ full-time science writers are more likely to go along with the views of the majority of conservative, "establishment" scientists than those of a dissenting minority. In nuclear physics, of course, the majority of scientists are employed by either the government or the utilities and are loath to bite the hand that feeds. Indeed, many of these scientists had attacked Sternglass viciously during an earlier controversy over atomic bomb test fallout, and extensive efforts had been made to discredit him.

Some news media may have had more direct reasons not to report news that could hurt the nuclear industry. One Pennsylvania television station was owned by a company that manufactures nuclear reactors, and the board of directors of a major daily that covered the accident included a former governor of Pennsylvania, whose son was a member

The Silent Toll

'Let neither men nor beasts, oxen nor sheep,
Taste any thing;
Let them not feed,
Nor drink the water . . . . "

— The Prophecy of Jonas

By Thomas Pawlick

"Those bastards! They're lying through their teeth! Look at these numbers . . . ."

Dr. Ernest J. Sternglass, briefcase thrown open on the seat beside him, clipboard balanced on his knee, furiously jots a stream of figures on a scrap of paper as the Yellow Cab, its bulbous, urban-tank-style body lurching on a set of rock-hard shock absorbers, races through the decomposing streets of Pittsburgh. Jolted by one of the city's abysmal potholes, the taxi's suspension recoils sharply, disarranging briefcase and clipboard and threatening to unseat the scientist.

Oblivious to the jarring ride and the grumblings of the cabbie, Sternglass is absorbed by the report he is reading; columns of numbers flow from his ball-point pen, and, if ever a man was seen riding an adrenalin rush brought on by a sheet of statistics, he is sitting in this cab. The pen pauses briefly, a series of figures are punched into a pocket calculator, and the excitement of the mathematical hunt builds.

"Look at this," he says with finality, jabbing the pen at his calculations. "They're liars. It's out-and-out misrepresentation. They say there is

no higher rate of hypothyroidism in infants in Pennsylvania, compared with other states, after Three Mile Island. But there is – it's right here in the statistics. Look at Montana . . . ."

The cab driver, made curious by the impassioned voice in his back seat, steals repeated glances at his passengers in the rearview mirror. Already Sternglass, having dropped his verbal composure in the heat of the search, has gained more genuine interest from this nameless cabbie than he will get from the radio, television and newspaper interviewers at the press conference to which he is heading.

Speaking with zeal, but with his scientific mask in place and choosing his words with care for the public record, Sternglass will lay a story of inestimable importance before Pittsburgh's media, and this media – bored, out of its depth and doubting this strange voice in the medical wilderness – will turn its back.

What Sternglass will tell them, using the government's own statistics, is that the near-meltdown of a nuclear reactor at Three Mile Island, near Harrisburg, Pennsylvania, is having demonstrable health conse-

quences in North America. He would tell them, if asked, that the constantly repeated public relations statement: "No one died at Three Mile Island" is untrue; he would, if asked, show them the statistics to prove it. Chances are good, Sternglass knows, that they won't ask, but he is here to give them the chance, nonetheless.

"O.K. This is the place," says the cab driver, bumping to a halt in front of a dingy storefront on Penn Avenue. The number is 938 and a sign reads: UNITED MINE WORKERS UPSTAIRS.

Union men in T-shirts and jeans watch curiously as the business-suited doctor makes his way quickly to a time-worn elevator which does not inspire trust. Moments later, the folding steel gate opens onto the second floor foyer, where a young woman with a tape recorder awaits with scarcely concealed impatience. A reporter for a local radio station, she is on her way to another assignment and has no intention of waiting for the scheduled press conference here to begin. Immediately, with neither fanfare nor introduction, she pokes a microphone into Sternglass' face.

News that the nuclear accident at Three Mile Island, Pennsylvania, may not have been as harmless as the plant owners claimed was first broken in Harrowsmith *Magazine in June 1980.*

of the state administration in power at the time of the accident. The son actually helped direct the state's investigation, which concluded that no one was hurt and endorsed the resulting written government report. It would be difficult indeed for a daily paper with his father on its board to say that the report was worthless.

As *Harrowsmith* publisher James Lawrence later wrote: "It would be an understatement to say that Ms. Watson's letter had taken on new importance." Obviously, if what Sternglass said was true, a major news story was being ignored, a story with international implications of the gravest sort. But equally evident, if Sternglass was wrong a lot of effort and expense might have to be put out by the staff before we could be sure of it. By following up, the magazine might pull off an enviable journalistic coup, but it could also end up looking like a publicity organ for crackpots.

An editorial conference was held, and it was decided that I should do some further checking. If what I found was positive, we would go to Pennsylvania and start snooping. If, on the contrary, it looked as if Sternglass were crying wolf, we would drop the story immediately. Unfortunately, there didn't seem to be much time for checking. Anyone could stumble on a story of this magnitude at any time and, especially if the stumbler was a daily newspaper, rush it into print long before *Harrowsmith,* with its publication lead time of a month and a half, could meet its deadline.

For all *Harrowsmith* knew, we might even then have been in a race, and spending too much time on a thorough backgrounding could have lost it for us.

Sternglass shuttled each week by plane from one job as a professor of the history and philosophy of science at Indiana University in Bloomington to another job as a radiation physicist at the University of Pittsburgh. I telephoned him in Pittsburgh and asked him to repeat his thesis, backing it up with figures taken from public health vital statistics records that I could verify for myself in any reference library. The names of other scientists who could support Sternglass' contentions were also provided when I asked, and some of them I recognized as highly respected in their fields.

Sternglass himself was an impressive and persuasive talker whom I instinctively trusted. The internal logic of what he was saying was too consistent to be the ranting of a fanatic. Although, objectively speaking, there was still insufficient reason to do so, I made a decision on the spot. "I'm coming to Pittsburgh," I said. "When and where can I meet you?"

Within forty-eight hours an airplane ticket had been purchased and a wad of traveler's checks issued. Jamming a few clothes, a notepad, tape recorder, camera, and spare cassettes into a small bag, I flew south to the City of Steel on the Monongahela River. Before the flight, appointments had been made with several other key people in the story, a list of questions to be answered had been drawn up, and a rough plan of action had been blocked out.

Jovial Jonas

Sternglass greeted his visitor in a cramped, book-lined office on the fourth floor of Presbyterian University Hospital, wearing a slightly threadbare white lab coat and a friendly grin. On the door to the hallway leading to his office a large sign bearing the international symbol for radiation was mounted, warning: "Danger—Radiation."

That sign was a fitting introduction. In a series of interviews over the next few days, Sternglass outlined a scenario of steadily growing danger, injury, and death of frightening proportions. The ultimate implications of what he said were outright horrible.

Yet Sternglass himself was a naturally jovial extrovert, full of energy and, hearteningly, of hope. An orthodox Jew, he thought of himself as a kind of modern-day Jonas, escaped from the belly of the nuclear industry whale for which he had once worked and come to warn the people of Nineveh to change their ways before disaster struck them down, the disaster in this case being nuclear.

In his wallet he carried a newspaper clipping, tattered but carefully folded and preserved, from the Washington *Post,* dated April 14, 1979. He waved it like a battle flag before troops. "This is an article by Bill Curry," he said. "I'll read it for you. It says: 'Officials involved in the U.S. atomic bomb tests feared in 1965 that disclosure of a secret study linking leukemia to radioactive fallout from the bombs could jeopardize further testing and result in costly damage claims, according to documents obtained by the Washington *Post.* The documents also indicated that the Public Health Service, the nation's top health agency, which conducted the study, joined the Atomic Energy Commission in reassuring the public about any danger from fallout.' "

Sternglass leaned forward in his chair: "You simply substitute the words 'Three Mile Island' and 'radioactive releases' for the terms 'bomb tests' and 'fallout,' and I believe we are facing essentially the same situation. The same kind of thing is going on with regard to releases from nuclear reactors as happened in the case of fallout from atomic bomb tests. To admit the health effects would lead to adverse public reaction, lawsuits, and the jeopardizing of the programs for further reactors. And so there is a cover-up."

Sternglass had made a careful study of the vital statistics records following the Three Mile Island accident and come up with some startling findings. He had examined regions that had been in the path of the radioactive clouds from TMI (the U.S. National Oceanic and Atmospheric Administration had prepared maps showing the pathways from March 28 through April 4, 1979) and compared them with regions that had not been in the clouds' route.

He had already reported the results in a paper delivered at a scientific conference in Israel, but the news media had failed to pick it up. "An examination of the monthly changes in infant mortality in Pennsylvania and the nearby areas of upstate New York as given in the U.S. Monthly Vital Statistics reports indicates that the mortality rate rose significantly shortly after the Three Mile Island accident in the directions where the plume of radioactive gases was known to have moved," Sternglass said.

"The number of reported infant deaths per month rose from a minimum of 141 in March of 1979 just before the accident to a peak of 271 in July, declining again to 119 by August. This is an unprecedented and highly significant rise of 92 percent in the summer months when infant mortality normally reaches its lowest values.

"In the four-month period following the accident, there were 242 infant deaths above the normally expected number in Pennsylvania and a total of about 430 in the entire northeastern area of the United States." While officials were insisting that the accident had killed no one, Sternglass' reading of the vital statistics provided strong evidence that at least 430 babies had been killed. It was a shocking claim.

In addition, Sternglass pointed to statistics gathered from the Morbidity and Mortality Weekly Report published by the U.S. Center for Disease Control in Atlanta, Georgia. These showed that, while infant death totals declined in cities such as New York and Philadelphia that were not in the gas clouds' path, those for cities in the path of significant emissions went up sharply. Thus, while infant deaths in Philadelphia declined by 18 percent and in New York by 6 percent from the total for July 1978 to the total for July 1979, the average number of infant deaths for that month in Pittsburgh, Syracuse, Albany, and Rochester actually *doubled* after the accident.

Sternglass could point to other statistics as well, such as the number of recorded cases of a disease called hypothyroidism. A malfunction of the growth-regulating thyroid gland, this disorder can be caused by the absorption by a child's thyroid of radioactive iodine-131, a substance that was released into the air in massive proportions during the TMI accident. Records revealed by another scientist, former Pennsylvania Secretary of Health Dr. Gordon MacLeod, showed an unexpected increase in the number of cases of hypothyroidism in the regions downwind of TMI after the reactor disaster. This disease is particularly dangerous to growing children, because the rate at which they grow is dependent on the correct functioning of the thyroid gland. If the gland malfunctions at one critical point, it can disrupt the growth of the child's brain, making that baby an idiot.

Along with these statistics, Sternglass also provided a list of references to the work of numerous scientists who had made experimental or statistical studies in the past showing how dangerous radiation—even very small amounts—was to living things. He advised me to read what these scientists had published and to talk to them personally, if possible. On the university's Xerox machine he ran off a thick pile of documents and handed them to me to study.

By this time I had become convinced of my original hunch that Sternglass was sincere and not a crackpot. He also seemed to have considerable objective evidence to prove his point. Nevertheless, it was still too soon to conclude that he *was* right, that he could not in all sincerity be mistaken. Before such a conclusion could be drawn, the scientific papers he had recommended would have to be read and digested, other scientists interviewed, and his opponents—the federal and state government authorities and public health officials—questioned for their side of the story.

In addition, Sternglass had made a fascinating suggestion. Any nuclear reactor that leaked would constitute a health danger for the people living around it, he said. It would not take a massive accident like that at TMI to affect the local statistics. Some reactors emit enough "hot" gases and liquids in normal operation to be fatal to babies. Why not pick a reactor *other than* the one at TMI and check the local health statistics for ourselves? There was a specialist in epidemiology (the study of the incidence and control of disease) right there at the university who could give advice, Dr. Thomas Mancuso, and a statistician named Dr. Rosalie Bertell in Buffalo, New York, who could be asked to help interpret whatever we found.

Most of the interviews with Sternglass over the past few days had been conducted in his office, but the one in which this suggestion was made was conducted over a couple of beers in a local bar frequented by university students and their professors. Perhaps it was the influence of the beer, but the idea of the magazine's conducting its own independent study seemed more attractive than intimidating. At least, such a study should ease our uncertainty as to whether Sternglass was right or wrong in his reading of the statistics.

A long-distance call was placed from my hotel room to the offices of *Harrowsmith,* and it was agreed that we should try it. One of the copy readers on our staff was a graduate medical librarian, and two other part-time staffers could be freed to help her gather material. Accordingly, the trio of researchers set to work looking up the records of radioactive emissions from nuclear reactors nearer home and the health statistics for the regions affected.

Dishonest Defense

A series of interviews followed. In Pittsburgh, I met with Dr. Gordon MacLeod, with Dr. Mancuso, and several more times with Sternglass. The mound of papers and documents to read and study grew deeper, as did my suspicions of the official "no one died" government line.

Later, when I flew to Harrisburg, scene of the accident and also the capital of Pennsylvania, those suspicions would turn to outright anger at the dishonesty of those attempting to defend the claim that the reactor breakdown had not affected anyone's health. The anger became open disgust when the unsavory backgrounds and conflicts of interest of those involved were revealed.

The opposite reaction was produced, however, by Dr. MacLeod. A careful, conservative medical doctor who specialized in public health, MacLeod was the very picture of scientific respectability. Highly regarded in his field, he had been selected by Governor Richard Thornburgh to be Secretary of Health to lend an air of respectability to the governor's cabinet. MacLeod even insisted that he was "definitely not" against nuclear power.

Nonetheless Dr. MacLeod, who had been Secretary of Health at the time of the TMI accident, was convinced that government officials were trying to cover up the health effects of the reactor breakdown.

"The [Pennsylvania] health department is being exceedingly restrictive with regard to the release of data [namely, statistics from the TMI area]," he said. "After I left the department I was called by former colleagues still working there and told about infant death statistics that had been compiled for an area in a five- and ten-mile radius of the reactor. These statistics showed that the rate of infant deaths had risen five times over what it had been in previous years. I asked if the department was going to release the data to the public and they said 'no,' and I was profoundly dismayed."

The same thing had happened with statistics showing an increase in the number of hypothyroidism cases downwind of the reactor. "They knew about the hypothyroidism data from October of 1979, and it wasn't until three months later that the public and the medical profession were alerted," MacLeod said, adding that the data held back by the government showed a *twelvefold* rise in hypothyroidism in one downwind county.

Calling the holding back of such information "unconscionable," Dr. MacLeod said his greatest concern had been that any babies suffering from thyroid gland problems caused by exposure to radioactivity should be treated "as soon as possible to prevent them from becoming cretins." If statistics showed that many children might have suffered such thyroid damage, area doctors should have been alerted to the danger and warned to look for the symptoms of hypothyroidism. Holding back the truth, he said, could possibly have doomed to idiocy children who might otherwise have been treated and saved.

Not until MacLeod himself made these facts public in a speech at a Pittsburgh church, however, did the state release any information. When the health department finally did break its silence, it was only to attack MacLeod and attempt to confuse the issue by comparing the statistics in question with other, irrelevant data. MacLeod provided copies of all of the statistics in question, which I was later able to compare with state health department news releases. MacLeod's story was true.

That, however, was only the beginning. It turned out that MacLeod had actually been fired from his post as Secretary of Health by Governor Thornburgh, and the circumstances of the firing were even more disturbing. Separate interviews with MacLeod and with the governor's press aide revealed what had happened.

After the accident, Governor Thornburgh had set up a commission—which included MacLeod as a member—to investigate the disaster and make a report. The commission's findings were to be given not only to Thornburgh but also to the federal group ordered to investigate the accident by President Jimmy Carter: the Kemeny Commission.

Among the documents gathered, MacLeod said, was an environmental report presented by the Pennsylvania Department of Environmental Resources which "was full of errors, misstatements and misrepresentations" and which failed to mention a second, and larger, release of radioactive iodine that took place after the first reactor accident.

Worried that the Kemeny Commission was receiving incorrect information from the state, MacLeod complained to the head of the Department of Environmental Resources and also wrote to the federal commission to inform its members of the mistakes. He had insisted from the start that all details of the accident should be made public and that those details should be accurate.

Within days, without any explanation, MacLeod was called to the governor's office and told he was fired.

Shoemaker's Job

Sternglass was safe from being fired for speaking out because of his status as a tenured professor at the University of Pittsburgh, and because royalties on his patents in X-ray technology had helped make him financially independent.

"Very early in my life, as a student at Cornell University, I had a fortunate opportunity to meet Albert Einstein, and he warned me to be careful," Sternglass said. "One of the things Einstein told me was to always have what he called a 'shoemaker's job,' a job where you can face yourself, doing something useful, where you can earn a living doing standard kinds of things and you don't have to be a genius every morning and have a great idea that will change the universe.

"I have tenure at the university, my work in X-ray technology, where I hold several patents, and financial security. So I have my shoemaker's job and can get controversial where other scientists existing on grants or at the whim of a university can't."

This information was a relief to me, as I had seen on past stories how easy it was for someone who spoke out in the press to suffer reprisals. As a matter of personal conscience I had warned Sternglass that if he was vulnerable he could still back out of the interview and I would print nothing. Better to lose part of a story than to cost someone his job. "Don't worry," he said. "There's no way they can get to me."

Indeed, "they," meaning government officials and the nuclear industry, had already exhausted their possible means to "get" Sternglass. He had been attacked in the press and in scientific journals as a liar and a sloppy scientist (proof of the allegations was invariably lacking) for his earlier public stand on atomic bomb testing and fallout. A publisher had actually burned 25,000 copies of a book Sternglass had written in 1972 on low-level radiation, and articles he had written for scientific journals had been suppressed. He was regularly insulted and attacked in public by his enemies, but he rarely lost his temper.

About the only thing that had not been tried against him was violence. Probably because he was so well known to the scientific community, the fate reserved for murdered antinuclear activist Karen Silkwood or that hoped for by the would-be assassins who attacked Dr. Rosalie Bertell had never overtaken him.

The knowledge that such attacks had been made against MacLeod, Sternglass, and others had made me leery of their opponents, and later revelations only increased the feeling. For example, it turned out that the chief of the Pennsylvania Emergency Management Service at the time of the nuclear accident was retired U.S. Army Colonel Oran K. Henderson, the commander of the brigade of troops that had committed the infamous massacre of women and children at My Lai during the Vietnam War.

Members of Governor Thornburgh's cabinet and state officials included numerous Army officers and persons with extremely close connections to the nuclear industry. Thornburgh himself was a former advisor to the Mellon family, controllers of the Aluminum Company of America, a corporation that uses large quantities of nuclear-generated electricity in its factory operations. The potential for conflicts of interest among these people when they were charged with assessing and reporting damage caused by a nuclear accident was self-evident.

What really convinced me that Sternglass was on the right track, however, were the scientific papers and articles I was now reading. Some had been supplied by Sternglass, some I had found on my own. Sitting in a Pittsburgh hotel over the weekend, I pored over this material: articles by Dr. Thomas Mancuso, Dr. Alice Stewart, Dr. Irwin Bross, Dr. Abram Petkau, and many others.

Biological Tragedy

These scientists, virtually unknown to the general, nonspecialized public, had performed experiments and studied statistics and come up with fearful evidence that even radiation in extremely small doses— doses believed safe by authorities when the development of nuclear power began—could be the cause of cancer, leukemia, hypothyroidism, genetic damage, and a host of other ills. Humans, animals, and plants were all vulnerable to this danger.

Sternglass described what he thought was the likely mechanism by which low-level radiation harmed the body. The damage to body cells caused by radiation, he said, may be due to the presence of radioactive particles called "free radicals," specifically negatively charged free oxygen radicals. "If there are too many of these radicals present in a cell (as would be the case after a large radiation dose), they bump into each other and deactivate each other," he explained.

"In order to do the most damage to a cell, you should put them in one by one. A gradual, gentle radiation is thus far more deadly than one big zap. Each of the radicals goes to a cell and starts a little chain reaction that unzips the cell and makes it rancid like butter, and it disintegrates." Such destruction can not only cause deformities in unborn children but also hamper the production of antibodies required by living creatures to fight off viruses, bacteria, and cancer cells. In short, it can destroy the natural immunity to disease of a person, animal, or plant and cause massive epidemics.

The evidence was also clear that the young of every species—babies, kittens, or even sprouting plants—were most vulnerable to radiation damage because their smaller body organs required less radiation to result in injury than did the larger organs of adult creatures. Thus infants and young animals would be the first to suffer from fallout or nuclear plant leaks, although eventually all living things could fall victim. A worldwide biological tragedy could be the ultimate result.

It was enough to shake anyone's composure.

My arrival in Harrisburg, however, snapped me out of it. Aided by family friend, Patricia Louque, a Puerto Rican woman active among the city's Spanish-speaking people and aware of local politics, I began interviewing local people involved in the TMI accident and its aftermath. These included the director of the city hospital, Warren Preleznik, his wife (who was an antinuclear activist), a state representative, staff members at the state health department, and various medical doctors and area residents. A visit to the site of the nuclear plant itself, along with interviews with people living next to it, provided a feel for the local atmosphere, as well as the added treat of hearing a public relations representative of the utility describe how "nothing much had really happened" at Three Mile Island.

A visit to the state health department was especially interesting. Vital statistics needed to document the accident's aftermath, it turned out, would not be published routinely as in previous years, but would be "delayed" for several months. Some statistics were not available at all. As soon as the fact that I was a journalist was mentioned, health department employees tensed and an underlying feeling of hostility became discernible. A visit with a receptionist in the office of Dr. George Tokuhata, however, proved enlightening. Tokuhata was in charge of gathering and controlling the release of health vital statistics in the wake of the accident, and his receptionist was wary of the press. A state representative to whom I had spoken, however, had asked me to bring him a copy of any documents the department might give me, so I simply presented myself as the legislator's friend, "dropping by to see if you could supply him with these documents." No mention of my journalistic status was made.

The receptionist, relaxed and feeling "among the inner circle," began to talk about the TMI controversy in general and eventually about the statistics themselves. "They weren't originally intended for the public or the press," she said. "But some of the material was leaked. Somebody leaked the figures and we had to confirm them." Department officials, she noted, were furious that public health information had thus become available to the public.

Her comments were worth more, in revealing the mentality of the officials in charge, than any of the news releases and statistics she eventually gave me.

Also a giveaway of the kind of mentality involved in the story were the reactions to my questions of Tokuhata and other officials. A doctor at the U.S. Center for Disease Control in Atlanta, who had attacked Sternglass earlier and claimed that his data were faulty, was reached by telephone at his office in Atlanta. When evidence that his attack had been unwarranted was read to him over the phone, he hemmed and hawed and stumbled over his words. Finally, he put his caller on "hold" and fled. His secretary came on the line a few moments later and said: "Dr. Greenberg has been called away on an emergency." The whole conversation, captured on tape and witnessed by another reporter on an extension line, was pure comic relief. Dr. Tokuhata avoided hard questions by begging off. "We're getting into an involved discussion," he complained.

The people on Dr. Sternglass' side of the aisle were decidedly more willing to talk and straightforward in their answers than were their opponents in official circles. Government and industry spokesmen lied, stumbled over their words, or refused comment. In contrast, those who agreed with Sternglass that the accident had caused tragedy tended to be open, voluble, and often blunt.

Probably the bluntest of them all, next to Sternglass himself, was Jane Lee, a widow in the town of Etters. A dynamo of a woman, she lived on a dairy farm only a short distance from the reactor and had collected valuable records of health damage to animals in the region both before and after the accident. She had interviewed local farmers and veterinarians and obtained signed statements from them telling of possible radiation-induced stillbirths, abortions, and genetic defects among cows, horses, pigs, poultry, and other animals. Her collection also included photographs of the affected creatures, as well as of trees that had lost their leaves following the accident, even though it was high summer. Asked what she thought of official claims that all of these things were mere coincidence, she glared across her kitchen table and said: "Bull!"

By this time, I agreed with her.

I had obtained all the statistics that were then available, read the scientific literature, and talked to key figures involved on both sides of the controversy. My conclusion was that Sternglass was right, that people—children—*had* died at Three Mile Island and that the public had a right to know it. The Pittsburgh media—one television station was owned by a company that manufactured nuclear reactors—were not about to break the story, and neither was the New York *Times*. The *Times*, which had consistently claimed that the TMI incident was totally harmless to the population's physical health and had also gone to great pains to ridicule Sternglass and MacLeod, seemed hopelessly biased on the issue. Its managing editor, Seymour Topping, denied that members of the *Times'* board of directors had any influence over editorial policy, but the fact remained that two members of that board were former Pennsylvania Governor William Scranton and William F. May, a strong supporter of nuclear power. No conflict of interest may have existed, but the potential for one was there.

I mulled this on the plane flying back from Harrisburg, a flight that I unexpectedly shared with Governor Thornburgh himself, who was traveling with a retinue of aides and research staff to Pittsburgh for a meeting. No one in his party mentioned Three Mile Island, and I watched them in silence as we flew.

Canadian Casualties

On arriving back at the *Harrowsmith* offices, I found still more shocking information waiting. During the two weeks I had spent in Pennsylvania, our researchers had assembled records from a nuclear reactor in northern New York State, as well as health statistics for Frontenac County, Ontario, directly across the U.S./Canada border from the plant. (A U.S. reactor was chosen because emission records for these facilities are public information, whereas in Canada such figures are classed as secret. It would have been a lengthy, perhaps impossible, task to pry emission totals from a Canadian power plant.)

The records gathered showed that there had been unusually large emissions of radioactive gases and water effluents from the New York reactor in 1975 and 1976 and, during the same time period, a sharp rise in the infant death rate in Frontenac County. A visit to the local weather office, where we interviewed a government meteorologist (not telling him why we needed this information) and pored over his maps and charts, revealed that winds from the vicinity of the New York reactor blew over Frontenac County at least 20 to 25 percent of the time—enough to carry radioactive gases to Canada. Finally, we checked with the Frontenac County health department, which told us there were no known epidemics in the area at the time that could have caused the fluctuation in infant deaths.

It was still not certain that the emissions and infant deaths were related, however, because the population of the county was small and the laws of statistics generally require large data bases to admit conclusions. To be surer of what we had found, I sent the figures off to biostatistician Dr. Rosalie Bertell in Buffalo—the same Dr. Bertell whose life had been threatened earlier.

She examined the figures and told us: "The evidence is not mathematically conclusive by itself, but it certainly is enough to warrant further study by the proper health authorities in Canada." It was possible that the leaky New York reactor had caused Canadian casualties, specifically an increase from 19 to 26 infant deaths for every thousand live births in the county in the year in question.

We published the story in the June 1980 issue of *Harrowsmith*. It was the cover story and received wide publicity all over North America and the world. Newspapers and radio and television stations in Canada, England, Japan, Europe, and many U.S. states picked up the story and added to it with interviews of the key persons involved. A Tokyo magazine translated the entire article into Japanese and published it.

The only place where the story was not picked up or discussed was in Pennsylvania. The news media there effectively ignored it.

Controversy over the story continued long after publication. Representatives of the nuclear industry in the U.S. and Canada both attempted to lessen its impact, smear its protagonists, or find mistakes in the article itself. Scientists employed by government or nuclear firms wrote letters, spoke on radio, and all but stood on their heads to convince people that the issue had no importance.

The article, however, had been written with extreme care—fear of libel always uppermost in the editors' minds—and was exceptionally well documented. The magazine was able to defend itself on every point and was never forced to retract or alter a single word. Typical of the letters to the editor it drew was that from cancer specialist Dr. Mark T. Goldberg of the Ontario Cancer Institute:

"Thank you for exposing the lie that no one died at Three Mile Island," he said. That statement said it all.

Overall, the article was successful in both its aims and the method of its production. The heaviest work involved and the most important was in the backgrounding and, later, in the writing. Both phases involved wrestling with exceptionally complicated and technical scientific literature, which demanded careful interpretation to make the concepts it dealt with intelligible to the reader. Nuclear scientists, also, seemed the ones most likely to attack the story, and errors of scientific fact would provide too easy an opening.

As an added protection in this regard, I sent copies of the draft article to Sternglass, MacLeod, and others to review for scientific accuracy. Only after their corrections had been inserted was the copy allowed into print. The finished story was proofread personally by the publisher as well as myself.

Follow-ups included stories in a subsequent issue describing the reactions of the people of Harrisburg and environs to the accident. These color stories, highly emotional in tone and character, showed that the psychological effects of the disaster were almost as serious as the physical ones.

The major disappointment arising out of the effort was the failure of other news media to follow up on what we had started by doing in-depth investigations of their own, either of the TMI incident or of the health effects of reactors in their regions. Only *The Village Voice* in New York and the *Sunday News-American* in Baltimore conducted serious inquiries, both begun before the *Harrowsmith* story appeared and neither focusing on health per se. The rest of the press in the U.S. and Canada let the issue drop after carrying the wire service version of our article or conducting cursory interviews with Sternglass or MacLeod.

Nuclear reactors can be found in nearly every region of North America, and in most cases their emission reports are on public record. Health statistics (except in Pennsylvania, recently) are also available to the public in most places, and nearly any university math department has statisticians on staff. It would be a simple matter for a paper to check local statistics to see if other reactors have produced fatal effects.

Up to the time this chapter was written, however, no one had done so.

Chapter IX

HIDDEN NAZIS

The physical and spiritual damage wrought upon the peoples of Europe during World War II by the followers of Adolf Hitler has never been equaled in horror. While vast armies fought across the ruined continent, millions of innocent civilians—Russians, Jews, Poles, and Gypsies—were systematically brutalized and slaughtered in concentration camps as part of the Nazi genocide program.

When the war finally ended with the Axis powers' defeat in 1945, the authors of these crimes—the war criminals who had murdered, tortured, maimed, stolen from, or performed hideous medical experiments upon their prisoners—suddenly saw retribution approaching. Panic ensued and an exodus began.

Although a tiny percentage of those responsible for the crimes were captured and tried by the Allied powers at Nuremberg, by far the greatest number got away scot-free. Most went underground in Germany, using false names, or fled to sanctuary in such Latin American havens as the Argentina of Dictator Juan Péron or the hinterlands of Brazil and Venezuela. But a handful of these outcasts fled to other countries, including both the United States and Canada.

Thus the war's final irony for some of those who had been its victims came after the shooting stopped. Anxious to forget the bitter memory of European tragedy, many death camp survivors reached North America only to discover that those who had persecuted them at home had immigrated with them. Their neighbors in the New World for the next thirty years would be their former oppressors from the Old World.

How this tragic situation came to be and what it meant in terms of human suffering came home to me in 1975, when the Montreal *Gazette* agreed to let me embark upon a hunt for hidden Nazis in Canada—a hunt that turned into a journey down a nightmarish version of Memory Lane.

Malpractice Case

The search was originally sparked by a malpractice case involving a physician who loudly proclaimed himself to have been a victim of

Nazi persecution. The doctor's tale of his wartime adventures in occupied Europe, which included a thrilling escape from a concentration camp and an emotional reunion with American troops, had been used to good advantage by his lawyers to gain the court's sympathy. Parts of his story, however, seemed a bit too theatrical and when, partly out of idle curiosity, I began to check out the details, possible discrepancies appeared. Similar discrepancies turned up in the background of one of the doctor's nurses, a Dutch woman who claimed to have earned her nursing degree in Germany during the war. According to Dutch authorities, only collaborators with the Nazis could have studied in Germany while the conflict was going on.

Whether the stories of the doctor and his nurse were entirely truthful posed an interesting question, but much more fascinating ones suggested themselves as my background checking progressed. What if there were not only one or two, but many collaborators, or even former Nazis, in Canada? What if actual mass murderers like Adolf Eichmann were living in Montreal, side by side with the very Canadians whose armies had helped defeat Hitler? What of the condition of the survivors of the wartime camps? How many were living in North America? Did they know of any war criminals living here?

The more one thought about these questions, the more intriguing they became. In my spare time (I had not yet been assigned the story) I began reading everything available on war criminals and the death camps of World War II, starting with the paper's clip files and working outward from there. On the bus going to work, at lunch hour, even at home in the evening, I pored over history books, memoirs, and yellowed clippings from the newspapers of thirty years ago. Local libraries and Montreal's multilingual bookstores provided an initial wealth of research material, the bibliography of each volume pointing the way to still more titles in both English and French.

The unfolding story of the camps was as absorbing as it was horrible, and it had by no means ended in 1945. Particularly valuable in understanding it all were *Les Criminels de Guerre (The War Criminals),* by Philippe Aziz; *Aftermath,* by Ladislaus Farago, and *The Swastika and the Maple Leaf,* by Lita-Rose Betcherman. Aziz' book described the most common escape routes followed by fleeing war criminals, showed how they financed themselves in their new homes, and gave a detailed list of the names and whereabouts (where known) of the most infamous among the fugitives.

Farago wrote of the hunt for Hitler's deputy, Martin Bormann, in Latin America and introduced the reader to the sinister organized crime syndicate of ex-Nazis and their friends known by the code name ODESSA. The existence of ODESSA gave the subject added relevance for postwar readers, who might otherwise have been tempted to think

50 war criminals alleged in Canada

DEC 26 1975

By THOMAS PAWLICK
of The Gazette

Germany - War Crime

More than 50 accused or convicted war criminals are living in Canada, groups seeking their capture charge, and until recently there was little hope any would be brought to justice by reluctant authorities.

Of the 50, whose names appear on various wanted lists already circulated through the federal bureaucracy without result, at least five accused criminals live in Montreal.

Several persons actually convicted abroad as war criminals have lived for years — with the government's knowledge — in Toronto, Winnipeg and other Canadian cities.

One of these persons may be called to account, in the near future, thanks to a still-confidential investigation aimed at proving violations of Canadian immigration law. If the evidence is sufficient, deportation could result.

If this happens, it will mark the first time the federal government has taken positive action on a war criminal's case, but probably will not bring any basic change in the attitudes of authorities.

As an immigration department spokesman said recently, commenting on a different case: "If such a person were to be deported.

The Second World War's legacy of bitterness remains.

Victims, or their kin, are still seeking justice for persecution committed by the Nazis living in Canada.

They live well, too, but may not be free from the law even here, says this article — the first of a two-part series.

---

it would have to be for reasons other than having been accused of war crimes. The war crimes would likely be only incidental."

Most alleged war criminals here are non-Germans who immigrated in the Cold War period, when Western governments, more worried about Communist agents than Nazi fugitives, did not ask about war crimes in their immigration screening.

The majority were granted Canadian citizenship, several have become wealthy and some are involved in politics or employed by government. None has yet served a prison term for his alleged offense, on which by international agreement there is no statute of limitations.

Efforts to bring them to justice have been mainly the work of private citizens, many of them former victims of the Nazi camps and ghettos, who work on shoestring budgets in hopes of gathering enough evidence to convince the government to take action.

They spend their own time and money, and in some cases risk physical danger. A Canadian agent for Austrian Nazi-hunter Simon Wiesenthal was once threatened with a loaded pistol by an accused criminal. They work because, as Sidney M. Harris, president of the Canadian Jewish Congress, put it in 1974:

"We are not prepared to sit idly by as fellow citizens any persons who may be proved in fact to have been guilty of war crimes against Jews or any other persons. This is one crime that time cannot heal."

Their ability to escape retribution and prosper is particularly galling to the thousands of concentration camp survivors living here now, who still suffer mentally, physically and often financially from their ordeals.

Failure to prosecute such persons even if a trial might prove them innocent, creates a dangerous precedent, as Montrealer Aba Beer a Janowska camp survivor, explains.

"Justice is not just to put Mr. X or Mr. Y in jail," he says. "The dead will stay dead regardless.

"The value of putting them in jail is that anyone who has similar ideas will hesitate

because he knows he'll be brought to account. If you don't do it, you make it easier for other dictators to think they can get away with it too, with another set of victims. Look at My Lai, or the Greek colonels."

History, however, gives those seeking justice reason to be skeptical, as the case of former Hungarian police Colonel Imre Finta, now a Toronto resident, illustrates.

Finta, who has been convicted in absentia of war crimes by a Hungarian court, came to Canada as an immigrant in 1951 and is now a Canadian citizen.

His case became widely known here in October, 1974, when Simon Wiesenthal accused him in a statement in Vienna of being responsible for the deportation of thousands of Jews from the ghetto at Szeged, Hungary, to Auschwitz, where most of the victims died.

Finta denied the accusation, saying: "I swear by my mother I never knew Hungarian Jews were sent to Auschwitz." He said the Szeged ghetto was the responsibility of German storm troopers, and his police worked only in the suburbs and country, not the cities.

After a brief sojourn in the headlines, the story died. But Wiesenthal and those working with him here continued to seek new evidence and pressed the Canadian government to open an investigation of his case.

Wiesenthal sent a letter to Canadian ambassador to Austria, J. A. Beesley, Oct. 10, 1974, outlining his accusation against Finta

---

'The value of putting them in jail is that anyone who has similar ideas will hesitate because he knows he'll be brought to account.'

---

and enclosing copies of written testimony from two Szeged survivors concerning his actions during the war.

On Nov. 6, 1974, Wiesenthal sent Beesley a signed affidavit form another Szeged survivor now living in Vienna, who said under oath:

"Police captain (later Colonel) Imre Finta, who had previously been at the ghetto of Nagyvarad, became commander of the (Szeged) ghetto. When Eichmann's staff in Budapest started to deport Jews to the camp in Auschwitz, a collaborator of Eichmann, SS-Hauptsturmfuhrer Franz Abromeit, together with Finta, organized the deportations."

The survivor's parents were deported in a later round-up and were "burnt alive" in a barracks in Gostling, Austria.

On Nov. 18, 1974, Wiesenthal sent Beesley the bill of impeachment from the Hungarian trial that convicted Finta dated 1947, in which further charges were detailed.

In Canada, Al Cutler of the Jewish War Veterans of Canada wrote Manpower and Immigration Minister Robert Andras about the case Nov. 21, 1974.

He received a reply Dec. 18 from Andras' departmental assistant, R. A. Button, saying: "This department has no record of Mr. Finta, except for the record of his original admission to Canada."

He added: "Mr. Finta is now a Canadian citizen and under present Canadian immigration law, out of our jurisdiction."

This reply was technically correct. By law, as a spokesman for the immigration department's appeals and litigation division explains: "No Canadian citizen can be deported. It is extremely difficult even to deport a non-citizen who has been here five years and established domicile.

The story of how Nazi war criminals escaped justice and found haven in North America was an emotionally difficult article to research. It appeared in the Montreal Gazette in 1975.

of the Nazi era as a closed chapter in history. The ODESSA had begun as a people-smuggling organization to help spirit former Nazis, mostly SS men, to hiding places around the world. Enriched by the stolen wealth of the SS and Gestapo, however, the group gradually evolved into a crime network similar in many ways to the Mafia, the Chinese Triad societies, and North America's drug-peddling motorcycle gangs. It engaged in illegal activities ranging from drug pushing, loan sharking, and prostitution to contract murders, and its influence was growing.

Betcherman's book described the Canadian fascists and Nazi sympathizers who had been active in Montreal, Toronto, and Winnipeg during the 1930's and 1940's. One chapter provided a shock when it mentioned what seemed to be a familiar name: "A Nazi agent was at work among the German Canadians. Dr. Karl (or Emil) Gerhardt, an erudite and urbane German who 'dressed like Bond Street' had been assigned to start a Nazi organization . . . to spread the Nazi propaganda line in Canada."

The *Gazette's* day city editor and office manager was a German by precisely that name, who had been in Canada during the same era and who fit many of the details given by Betcherman. "It can't be, not Karl," I thought, and sure enough, it wasn't. The paper's editor spelled his name without a "t"—Gerhard, not Gerhardt—and had no connection whatever with the agent who had been his namesake. "Our" Karl had cut his ties with his native Germany not long after Hitler came to power and partly in reaction to the Nazis' excesses. He had become a Canadian citizen and helped many anti-Nazi prewar refugees from Europe find safety in Canada.

"I had a hell of a time when the other Gerhardt was active here," he recalled. "People thought I was him and I used to get all kinds of angry calls at the office." This brief mix-up over names turned out to be a valuable lesson, making me cautious and preventing me from jumping the gun later when I found several men in Montreal whose names matched those given on a Soviet Russian list of wanted war criminals. The presence or absence of a single letter in a German or Slavic name could make the difference between wasting time on a fruitless background check and researching the trail of a genuine suspect. It could also, obviously, make the difference between publishing the truth and printing an error that could bring a libel suit.

All of this reading was essential, not only in ascertaining the whereabouts of those war criminals who had not managed to disappear, but in getting a feel for the ideas and personality types that formed the Nazi movement. The task of tracking missing persons is always easier if the tracker has some idea of how the vanished quarry thinks. Thought precedes and governs action.

Reading alone, however, was unlikely to turn up any bona fide fugitives who had gone to ground. By now thoroughly hooked on the subject, I knew that I would have to get out on the street if this interest were not to remain merely academic. Eventually the paper's resources would be needed to make the search bear fruit, and to whet the editors' appetite for news something more tangible than history-book knowledge was required.

Litany of Lists

An excellent way to get information on a criminal is to talk to his victims. Unlike the police, the courts, or government bureaucrats, whose interest is detached and purely professional, the victims *care* about what happened. They remember every detail of every injury and usually nurse a vivid desire to see the malefactor get his due.

The Russians, who lost twenty million people in World War II, the Jews, who lost six million, and the Poles, who lost one million citizens, were the three leading victims of the Nazi scourge and hence most likely to remember details of that time of suffering. Unfortunately, information stemming from the Soviet government or its captive Polish satellite regime was not likely to be reliable. Colored by ideology and grinding whatever ax the Communist Party line of the moment demanded, their pronouncements on any subject would be suspect.

I decided to start with the Canadian Jewish Congress (CJC), which had offices in both Montreal and Toronto. In Montreal, I talked to CJC national executive director Alan Rose and builder Aba Beer; in Toronto I dealt with Benjamin Kayfetz.

Rose, a British Army veteran who had been present at the liberation of one of the death camps, was concerned and helpful but warned that not all members of the modern Jewish community would be eager to help root out war criminals. Others interviewed repeated similar warning notes. The present generation of Jews, who were not yet born when the Holocaust fell upon their parents, were more interested in Israel's battle to survive in the hostile Arab Middle East than in "dredging up the past" of wartime Europe. Some young people, ignorant of such heroic struggles as the Warsaw Ghetto uprising, actually felt ashamed of the Holocaust, mistakenly believing that the European Jews had not fought back or somehow deserved their fate.

As for the camp survivors themselves, some would certainly try to aid my search, but others would not want to reopen old wounds and would resent my questions. The hurt was so deep, the memory so painful that a stranger blundering in, full of clumsy curiosity, might not be welcome. An outsider would be well advised to go cautiously and use tact.

Rose explained that the CJC was aware of several accused or convicted war criminals living in North America and maintained a record of their names and addresses. The CJC list was based on information from a variety of sources, including camp survivors' organizations, the Israeli government, the Soviet and other East European governments, and from Simon Wiesenthal's Vienna-based Jewish Documentation Center. Each of these sources had a list of its own, a litany of the names of the accused and the accursed.

The lists were generally kept confidential, for the very good reason that making a suspected person's name public in the absence of conclusive proof of guilt could malign the reputation of an innocent person—or bring a libel suit upon anyone who accused him in print. Only the names of those who had actually been convicted of war crimes in a court of law, or against whom very substantial evidence had been amassed, were normally released.

Rose was nevertheless willing to provide initial information on a few suspects, including three accused men whose cases had already been made public: a Hungarian named Imre Finta and two Ukrainians, Dmytro Kupiak and David Geldiaschvilli. Geldiaschvilli had only recently been arrested by the Soviets while on an ill-considered trip home to visit his relatives, but Finta and Kupiak were living in Toronto.

"The German invaders often used local auxiliaries to do their dirty work in the countries they occupied," Rose said. "Thus you find numerous Ukrainian or Hungarian names on the war criminal lists. After the fighting stopped, the Cold War with Russia began and Canadian and American immigration people were more interested in keeping out Communists than in screening for ex-Nazis. In the case of German nationals, they did check their papers and for SS tattoos, but non-Germans were not very carefully checked.

"Lots of these people had very minor positions. They were just underlings to the Germans. Some of those coming over were also collaborators in name only. Some of the Ukrainian nationalists trying to gain independence from Soviet Russia cooperated militarily with the Nazis, and after the war the Russians labeled them war criminals. Politics came into play. The records of the Germans' local auxiliaries fell into the hands of the Russians, and they used them to make trouble whenever they were annoyed with Canada.

"Those accused by the Russians who actually were war criminals could not be sent back because the norms of justice of the Soviet regime were considered different than ours and our governments believed they would not get fair trials."

In the case of Geldiaschvilli, he said, Canadian government observers who had been present at his trial in the USSR regarded the evidence against him as "overwhelming" and believed the trial had been conducted "in a fair and proper manner." But there was no guarantee that all such trials would be equally fair. "These doubts are probably understandable," Rose added. As for Finta and Kupiak, the former had been convicted of war crimes in absentia by a Hungarian court, and the latter had been accused by the Soviet government but never tried.

Rose also supplied the names of three other accused men, two Ukrainians and one Rumanian. He mentioned no Germans.

Montreal builder Aba Beer, who had survived the infamous Janowska concentration camp, was also helpful when contacted. In fact, he became my best source and made a lasting moral impression upon me. His agony under the Nazis was described in Howard Roiter's *Voices from the Holocaust,* but he was surprisingly free of bitterness.

"Justice is not just to put Mr. X or Mr. Y in jail," he said. "The dead will stay dead regardless. The value of putting them in jail is that anyone who has similar ideas will hesitate because he knows he will be brought to account. If you don't do it, you make it easier for other dictators to think they can get away with it too, with another set of victims. Look at My Lai in Vietnam, or the Greek colonels. Capturing these people and putting them on trial is not vengeance. It is homage to the dead and a warning to the living."

Beer's chief emotion as he talked was not anger, but sadness: sadness that such things could happen, that so little had been done about it, that it would be so easy for it all to happen again.

"Right now we live very comfortably," he said. "But through history we've seen countries have their ups and downs. Danger would appear, and some kind of dictator would take advantage of it. Look what the Turks did to the Armenians.

"There is a girl [Karen Quinlan] in the United States now who is supposed to be medically a vegetable. She is supposed to be clinically dead, and her family is making a big thing out of wanting to disconnect the respirator. They are asking permission from the court to do it, when it is already accepted as the doctor's prerogative to disconnect it when a case is hopeless. Maybe they should pull the plug and let her go, if she's dead already, but why take it to court and publicize it?

"That's how it started in Germany. It started with hard cases and spread to anybody who was unproductive. They didn't arrest everybody right away. They did it gradually. Look at Nixon. How far would he have gone without the Washington *Post?*"

Beer's reasons for not wanting to bury the past just yet seemed more than reasonable—they seemed urgent and necessary. Sitting in the living room of his comfortable brick home, sipping coffee from delicate porcelain cups, we were a far cry from the barracks of Janowska, it seemed. But perhaps, given human nature and its weakness, we were not really so far. We moved on to the subject of evidence, of how a mass murderer might be convicted or why he would be left to run free.

"Some of our people [the camp survivors] are afraid to go and testify," Beer said. "It's nearly impossible to remember details that happened thirty years ago. A defense lawyer who puts you on the stand can make a fool of you, make you seem a liar. If he asks for dates, you may not know them. If they want you to identify a man, who may have been thirty and in uniform when you saw him last, how can you recognize him if he's now sixty-five, fat and droopy, and in civilian clothes? I wouldn't recognize my own brother after thirty years.

"They want witnesses. Where are you going to get two witnesses when they are all dead, gassed? Also, the courts in Europe are not too interested in such cases anymore. The Russians are, but they may have their own reasons for calling somebody a war criminal. They call all enemies of their regime fascists and so forth. Other European nations aren't interested, especially Austria."

Further interviews would show that the Canadian government was not interested either. As long as the crimes in question were not committed in Canada and those who perpetrated them did not enter the country illegally, Ottawa preferred to look the other way.

I was to have several more interviews with Beer, whose advice and background explanations were crucial. Eventually, with his cooperation, I obtained a copy of the Soviet wanted list, which Russian officials had given to the Royal Canadian Mounted Police without result. Thirty-four persons were named on it, all of them living in Canada.

Beer and the Toronto CJC's Ben Kayfetz were able to provide more information about Imre Finta and Dmytro Kupiak. They also supplied the name of Simon Wiesenthal's Toronto representative, who asked that his name be kept confidential, and several other people familiar with either the camps or the postwar movements of various criminals.

The cases of both Finta and Kupiak had been publicized a year earlier, when the Soviet government, stirred up by the Geldiaschvilli case, had asked for Kupiak's extradition. At the same time, Simon Wiesenthal had called on the Canadian government to deport Finta. By coincidence, both men made their living in Canada in similar professions. Finta had become a caterer and food consultant, and Kupiak owned a restaurant in Toronto. The Ukrainian had been a Conservative Party candidate for Parliament in the 1972 federal elections, garnering 9,000 votes but losing the election.

Wiesenthal charged that Finta, a former Hungarian police colonel who came to Canada in 1951 and subsequently became a Canadian citizen, had acted as a lieutenant to arch-murderer Adolf Eichmann during the war, commanding the Szeged Ghetto in Hungary and aiding Eichmann in the deportation of thousands of Jews to Auschwitz. When the story first broke in 1974, Finta had denied the accusation, saying: "I swear by my mother I never knew Hungarian Jews were sent to Auschwitz." Wiesenthal was quoted in the papers as promising to send proof of his charges to Ottawa, but nothing further on the case had been reported publicly in Canada.

Kupiak, who came to Canada in 1948, was accused by the Soviets of having led a band of the Organization of Ukrainian Nationalists under Stepan Bandera that killed 200 persons, including several Jews, while cooperating with the invading German army. Kupiak denied the charges, saying: "I never killed anyone except in battle with the Russian commissars and the NKVD (Soviet secret police)."

Time to Organize

How true were the charges against these two men? Were they really criminals or merely the object of political vendetta? Eventually, the question would have to be put to them—and the other suspects living in Canada—directly. But before that, more details of their backgrounds would have to be gathered and sifted.

It was obvious too that more than a superficial acquaintance with the sufferings and views of the camp survivors would have to be gained before a true perspective on the story could be achieved. The first interview with Beer had raised an important question in my mind. Was the assumption correct that criminals in hiding were the main news story, or was it possible that the fate of the fugitive Nazis was only half the story, that the full truth about their victims had never been told? (Doubt on this point eventually grew to a conviction that the survivors' tale had not been adequately told, and it resulted in a separate article.)

It was time to sit down and organize what had been found, to plan the next steps in the investigation, and to propose the story to the *Gazette* editors. I typed a memo to the city editor, explaining the subject and concluding: "It seems to me like a four-part series, as follows: 1) Former Nazis and collaborators in Canada—who are they, where are they, how did they get here, and were they ever punished? 2) Former Nazi camp victims—who are they, where are they, and what is their current status (rehabilitated, still suffering, what)? 3) What do the law and Canadian government say about war criminals? How come they are living here and have escaped punishment from a legal viewpoint, political one, and moral one? 4) Neo-Nazism—any signs of it in Canada, and how do former camp victims feel about it?"

The Geldiaschvilli case was still fresh in the public's mind, and a flurry of Nazi-hunting interest had recently taken place in the U.S. following publication of Farago's book on Martin Bormann. The city editor was interested and gave the go-ahead to start working on the story as a regular assignment. It was not my only assignment, however, and time to work on it would have to be sandwiched in between other stories. In the end, most of the work had to be done on my own time, but at least long-distance phone calls and taxi fare could be charged off on the expense account.

For my own use, I typed an outline of questions that needed to be answered, listing possible sources of information next to each question, and blocked out a rough order of procedure. I decided to attack the problem of locating the criminals first, to minimize the chances of grapevine gossip about my inquiries on other aspects of the subject getting back to some fugitive and tipping him prematurely.

It was unlikely that any genuine Nazi fugitive would make himself conspicuous by contacting known neo-Nazi extremist groups, such as George Lincoln Rockwell's American Nazi Party or the Toronto-based Western Guard. The kind of loonies such groups attracted could easily blow a hunted person's cover. But just to be sure I reactivated the post office box I had rented under an assumed name during the black market adoption story. Giving it as a return address, I wrote to several right-wing extremist groups, requesting their literature and asking how to join their group.

Predictably, this gambit produced no substantial leads, demonstrating only that the lunatic fringe was alive and well. The real work of the investigation was to depend on plain, dull legwork, on reading, research, and careful, detailed interviews with a few key people.

I made several trips to the Jewish Public Library in Montreal, where the staff guided my reading and provided titles, papers, and news clippings. Between library trips I went to the Russian, Polish, Dutch, and Israeli consulates and pestered their staffs. I wrote to Yad Vashem in Israel—a memorial shrine to the victims of the Holocaust, whose staff also maintains extensive archives of records from the war era—as well as to the authors of several books on the camps. Authors queried included Hermann Langbein (a former Auschwitz inmate who had written extensively on the camps' history), Conrad Baars (a former Dutch Resistance member), Professor Raul Hilberg, and famed psychoanalyst and former Auschwitz prisoner Viktor Frankl.

Both the Polish and the Russian consuls were willing to provide general information—published histories of the war, copies of official government statements on what constituted a war crime, and so forth. One of the books produced by the Russians, titled *Day of Reckoning*, gave the official Soviet version of the history of the Ukrainian independence movement, including a detailed description of the alleged crimes of Kupiak and other members of the Bandera group. There was, of course, no way to check its validity. When it came to more specific questions, however, neither consul was of much help. The Russian official denied any knowledge of the list of wanted men his government had given to the RCMP. (The Mounties would not release it either.)

I finally did obtain a copy of the Russian list from Aba Beer, who chuckled when he handed it over and saw the look on my face. It was in Russian, in the Cyrillic alphabet, which was total gibberish to me. Beer did not have time to translate the long list, which included biographical details after each name. "You'll have to scratch your head a little bit," he apologized. Fortunately, one of the copy editors at the paper, Matt Radz, was a Pole who could also read Russian. He translated the list, thus allowing my own head to remain unscratched.

Some of the names on the list were startling. Mostly Ukrainians, they included a priest, several prominent businessmen, and a high-level executive in the Canadian television broadcasting industry. A check through the clip files, however, showed that several of the persons named also were outspoken advocates of Ukrainian independence who had continued to be politically active after their arrival in North America. The Soviets would no doubt insist that this was mere coincidence, but it was obvious that none of the names could be published without some independent corroboration of the Russians' charges.

Pressed for either more names or more details on the Russian list, Alan Rose suggested that I talk to Kayfetz in Toronto and also to Wiesenthal's representative there. As we conferred, I noticed a file folder on Rose's desk, with what looked like a list of names in it. He left the room and I stole a quick look at the folder. The top document had the name Imre Finta typed on it, but before I could look further Rose came back in the office. The logical next step, evidently, was to go to Toronto.

Working on the limited budget allowed by the paper, however, would not permit many trips to Toronto. I decided that, to get the maximum mileage from this visit, I should try to interview any suspected war criminals living there whose names I had already obtained. Telephoned, Kupiak agreed immediately to an interview to defend his war record.

Finta, however, could not be reached. The Hungarian had withdrawn from public view following Wiesenthal's denunciation, changing his telephone to an unlisted number and refusing to speak to any stranger except through his lawyer. Other suspected criminals living in the area could not be reached in time to set up interviews before my scheduled flight.

Lonely Pursuit

Kayfetz, like Rose, was helpful, but only up to a point. It was Simon Wiesenthal's representative who turned out to be the more valuable contact. He was, like the legendary Austrian Nazi hunter himself, a former concentration camp inmate who had gone through his share of the agonies of the damned. It showed in his eyes as we sat talking in the cramped, dusty office of his wholesale warehouse in downtown Toronto.

A strangely quiet man who moved slowly and every now and then seemed to lose interest in the present, staring away into the distance, he nodded when asked about various suspects. Yes, he said, he knew this or that man. Yes, there was much evidence available, but it was all in Russia. None of the documents were available in the West. He seemed weary.

When I mentioned Finta, however, he came back to life. It was this sad-eyed man who had found Finta for Wiesenthal. "The newspapers here got many of the details wrong," he said. "They said he was a former police captain, but he was actually a colonel. We have affidavits from the victims, sworn and notarized, attesting to what he did." Noting that he had tracked the Hungarian for weeks, he smiled: "Once, when I talked to him, he actually pulled a gun on me and threatened to shoot me if I didn't leave him alone. I have been threatened many times, by many people.

"It is not always easy to be sure we have the right man, and sometimes we have to talk to them, get close to them. Right now, I am dealing with a German, a former higher-up in the party who has been living since the war in South America. He has a close relative living in Toronto and has taken a big chance to come here and visit him. He does not know who we really are, and I am trying to get his fingerprints on something so we can check with his file. Wiesenthal has it in Vienna. I tried to get his prints on a lighter, but it didn't work. This week, I'm to try to get them on a glass at a bar. If it works, and he is the man, we will ask the Canadian government to arrest him, as he is here illegally. He is a big name."

I was, naturally, fascinated, but he would not reveal the German's name. He showed me a picture, but I did not recognize it. The man in the photograph wore an SS uniform.

The quiet wholesaler, who spent virtually all of his nonbusiness hours relentlessly tracking Hitler's former followers, gave me Wiesenthal's address and telephone number in Vienna and suggested that I contact him for further documentation on Finta and the others. He also gave me a Toronto number that he believed was the unlisted number of Finta. He put the German SS man's photo back in a file on his desk and bade me goodby. I was no more than a temporary interruption on the path of his lonely pursuit. He had other fish to fry, other memories to exorcise.

Going out of his office, I deliberately left a glove on the floor near the chair where I had been sitting. As we walked through the warehouse, I pretended to suddenly notice its absence and told him I would go back to the office and get it. I walked quickly in and immediately tried to steal a look at the file folder on his desk, but the wholesaler read my thoughts. He followed me back to the office at a discreet distance and, just as I went to open the folder, called out: "Did you find the glove?" He came in, and I bent to pick up the glove. "Yes," I answered, "I found it." We exchanged looks. He knew I really hadn't found anything.

I hailed a cab outside and gave the driver the address of Dmytro Kupiak's restaurant. Having met the hunter, it was time to meet one of the hunted.

There was nothing noteworthy about the restaurant except that the main dining room was large, bare and open like a cafeteria, and the menu included several typically Slavic items: cabbage rolls and potato plotski (pancakes). In his photographs, Kupiak looked like a large man, with a long, jowly face and eyes set close to his nose. In person, he seemed much smaller, older and grayer. When I entered, he was sitting at a table talking to a customer, and I decided to eat before introducing myself. I ordered a plate of stuffed cabbage and studied him as I munched. Was he a war criminal, a monster?

He looked—ordinary. Sitting there in a checked sport coat, talking and gesturing, he seemed indistinguishable from any other good Tory Chamber of Commerce member. Of course, that may have been all he was, an immigrant businessman who had gotten on the wrong side of the Kremlin years ago.

After eating, I went over and said hello, shaking hands.

Except for his slight accent, Kupiak—"Call me Metro, everybody does"—was almost the stereotype middle-aged, conservative North American businessman. His politics stemmed from the Cold War era, and his social attitudes seemed roughly on a par with those of George Babbitt. The business of Dmytro Kupiak seemed to be business, plain and simple. At certain points in the conversation his eyes seemed to narrow with either calculation or suspicion, but this may have been only a natural suspicion of the news media.

I mentioned the names of his alleged victims, quoting from *Day of Reckoning,* and pressed him about his supposed crimes. I asked a question one way, then came back to it later in slightly different words, trying to see if his story would change. But Kupiak had been over the ground before. He had learned to speak to reporters during his earlier election campaign, and he had had more than a year to mull over the Soviet charges.

"I liquidated many of the Russian commissars during the fighting," he said. "But the only Jews I met were two that we beat up. They were Communist informers. Eight young men died because of them and my own parents were sent to Siberia, where my father froze to death. We took them to our headquarters and beat them on the ground, but did not kill them. If they had been Russians we would have shot them, but I told my men the Jews already had enough trouble on their heads and we spared their lives."

This, it seemed, was unusually generous behavior. Was he lying, or exaggerating—or was it true? There was no way to know. I left him in his restaurant, grinning effusively but uncomfortably at me as I went out the door. I had to hurry to catch the plane back to Montreal. Would all the suspects be this bland, I wondered?

Before finding out, it seemed a good idea to check with Wiesenthal to see what evidence he had collected on Finta and the mysterious German SS visitor. It would be well, also, to see if any of the queries that had been launched had turned up further details on other suspects. The Kupiak interview was disappointing. I felt that I had somehow not done my job with him, and I wanted to do better with the others.

Transatlantic Call

I had read a lot about Simon Wiesenthal, including his autobiography, and I was somewhat intimidated by his moral stature and past accomplishments. What would the man who had survived Auschwitz and lived to play a key role in the capture of Adolf Eichmann think of a brash and obscure young reporter? Would he even bother to speak to me?

I swallowed my misgivings and dialed the overseas operator, asking her to make a call to Vienna, Austria, to the Jewish Documentation Center. The phone rang, and a man's voice came on the line, asking: "Ja?" It was Wiesenthal himself. Feeling ignorant speaking English rather than German, I introduced myself and explained my business, adding that, after the original story announcing his accusations against Finta, nothing more had been heard. Did he have documentation to back up what he had said?

He did indeed. More than a year ago, he said, he had sent a letter outlining the charges against Finta to the Canadian ambassador to Austria, J. A. Beesley, including the original bill of indictment of the Hungarian court and affidavits from two Szeged Ghetto survivors testifying to Finta's role in the deportations to Auschwitz. He would send copies to me, he promised. I asked about the SS man in Toronto, but he claimed not to know whom his agent had been talking about. I pressed him, but to no avail. If he did know about the German, he was not about to say.

In due time an envelope containing the documentation on Finta came in the mail. Written replies from several other European and Israeli sources giving information on other accused criminals also began coming in, as did some interesting documents discovered in the course of routine rubbish pickups at the addresses of various suspects. (I had begun reading the rubbish of some of these persons—including the doctor and nurse mentioned previously—early in the investigation.)

According to the author of one signed affidavit, given to Ambassador Beesley in November 1974, Finta had been connected with more than one deportation effort in Hungary: "Police captain [later colonel] Imre Finta, who had previously been at the ghetto of Nagyvarad, became commander of the [Szeged] ghetto. When Eichmann's staff in Budapest started to deport Jews to the camp in Auschwitz, a collaborator of Eichmann, SS Hauptsturmführer Franz Abromeit, together with Finta, organized the deportations."

The survivors' parents were deported in a later roundup and were "burnt alive" in a barracks in Gostling, Austria.

I decided to telephone Finta, but checked an old Toronto phone book first to see if he was listed there under his pre-1974 number, and to note the address. I then telephoned the information operator, gave her the new, unlisted number I had obtained from Wiesenthal's man, and said: "Operator, I just dialed this number to get a Mr. Finta, who lives on [I named the street] and was told it wasn't a good number. Can you check it for me?" There was a pause, and the operator came back on. "Sir, that number is an unlisted number, but it is for that address and that name. We can't give out unlisted numbers, of course, but you already have the number so I guess it doesn't matter. It's the only Finta with that initial in my book."

Armed with the knowledge that I had the right number, I attached a tape recorder telephone pickup to the receiver, turned the recorder on, and dialed Finta's home. A woman answered, and I asked for Finta. "Who is this?" she asked, and I told her. "I'm sorry, but he isn't here. There is nobody here by that name," she said, and hung up. I tried again, but to no avail. If Finta was home, he was not talking to any strangers. His quotes of a year ago, denying Wiesenthal's initial charges, would have to stand as his only public defense.

A similar reluctance to come to the phone was exhibited by the other accused men. Unlike Kupiak, who seemed eager to prove his innocence, they were frightened, almost terrified by any inquiry. One Ukrainian named on the Soviet wanted list would not come to the phone, even when his wife (who had answered) urged him. "He'd rather not speak about it [whether he was a war criminal]," she said. "I can't get him to take the receiver."

Another accused Ukrainian, in his late 60's, came to the phone but grew more and more frightened as I questioned him. His voice shook. "No more," he said. "I think you better speak to our priest." He hung up. I phoned the Ukrainian parish priest, who told me: "He is old and frightened. He has had trouble with agents trying to scare him. He also doesn't speak English very well. You're wasting your time trying to talk to him." It was the same with all of them.

By now my list of names, from all sources, had grown to more than fifty but, except for Kupiak, all were frightened. None would talk frankly.

As for the doctor and nurse whose stories had originally sparked my curiosity, I found many suspicious things in their backgrounds, but nothing conclusive enough to stand up in print or in a libel trial. Unlike most camp victims, the doctor had no tattoo. But Dr. Viktor Frankl, himself a veteran of Auschwitz, admitted that he had no tattoo either. The dates in the local doctor's story seemed wrong in some places, but memory may have played tricks on him after thirty years. Other details of his story suggested that he might have been part of the Judenrat, the puppet ghetto government set up in various cities by the Germans to mollify the Jews until they could be shipped away to their deaths. Most of the Judenrat members were themselves Jews and would also be shipped away, but they were the last to go. The other ghetto residents frequently regarded them as turncoats. But being a member of the Judenrat or one of its assistants could also be evidence of heroism. Some members used their position to intercede for their fellows, saving many from the gas chambers.

As for the nurse, she would have been fairly young during the war; perhaps, if anyone was a collaborator, it might have been her parents. Perhaps there were mitigating circumstances of some kind. Recent letters from her parents in Holland contained cryptic references indicating that the parents kept at an oddly unexplained distance from their daughter's husband and children in Canada. They asked her to "please destroy" their letters and not show them to the grandchildren, adding, "give them a hug and kiss without them knowing who it is from."

In the end, however, nothing substantial could be found. Without more convincing evidence, I decided to forget the malpractice case and its defendants.

It was time to start meeting some of the Nazis' victims and hear their stories. Afterward I would also have to talk to government officials—to the immigration and justice ministries—to assess the legal problems involved in arresting or deporting war criminals, but that could wait. I wanted to know, to feel, what the Nazis had really done to people before dealing with the cold objectivity of the law.

Awful Memories

Beer and Rose put me in contact with the Association of Former Concentration Camp Inmates in Montreal, and also provided introductions to Dr. John Stahr and Dr. Erika Barber of the local office of the United Restitution Organization (URO), which represents Jewish camp victims in their efforts to obtain compensation claims from the West German government. The names of several non-Jewish survivors of the death camps were supplied by the Polish Canadian Congress, which put me in contact with the Polish association of camp survivors.

Their stories, and their current plight, were a profound shock. The URO offices were crammed with files, each one more tragic than the last. The memories these people had to live with were truly awful, in every sense of the word.

In January 1943, a young woman in childbirth was taken to a makeshift hospital in the Jewish ghetto of a German-occupied town in northern Poland. "I was delivered there of a baby boy," her file in the URO said. "Three or four days later, while the baby was nursing, a group of SS men came and began chasing people out of the hospital to be used for forced labor. My child was taken from me and killed by the SS in front of my eyes in a cruel way. I won't say in which way, because it is too cruel."

"She told me what she wouldn't write," added Dr. Barber. "An SS man, either a German or a Ukrainian, took the child by both legs and physically ripped it in two. This woman is today a nervous wreck. She is under constant medical care, suffers from bouts of terrible depression, and finds it difficult to keep her job."

Her application for restitution payments under a West German law passed in 1953 was at first refused, said Dr. Barber. The law covered only those who were "stateless persons" at the time it was passed, and in 1953 the young woman was a Polish citizen. She had immigrated to Canada afterward. After intervention by URO lawyers, she was eventually granted a single, lump-sum payment of $4,500.

Hundreds of other claimants, many of them physically or mentally ill and in financial need, hadn't been so lucky. Dr. Stahr explained why: "The West German indemnification law passed in 1953 was originally intended to last four years. But so many applicants came forward that it had to be extended several times. The last extension ended in 1965. Anyone who came forward with a claim after 1965 had missed the boat.

"For example, survivors of the ghetto in Kiev, in the Ukraine, were not stateless persons after the war but citizens of the Soviet Union, where they received no payments. Recently the Soviet government has allowed some Jews to emigrate to Israel and the West. A person in need coming from Kiev now is too late to apply for any benefits. There are hundreds of people like this in Montreal and perhaps thousands in the world."

After the 1965 deadline expired, the World Jewish Congress pressured the Bonn government for another extension of the law, and finally a compromise was reached. A bill was drawn up authorizing a fund of 540 million marks to be handed over to the Congress for distribution to survivors who had missed the deadline. But the man who was to guide the bill through the legislature died, and it was never introduced.

One former camp inmate who never received compensation was Czech resistance fighter Milos Witek, a Roman Catholic who had just graduated from law school when he was arrested by the Gestapo in 1941. He survived imprisonment in both Mauthausen and Dachau and emigrated to Canada after the war.

"The horrors of Mauthausen were beyond any imagination. They marked me," he said. "After the war I tried to bury myself in my work to forget, but the nightmares are still coming. I overcame the physical marks, but for a long time I was always frowning. It affects your family life."

Witek took part in resistance work in the camps and was responsible for saving the lives of many political prisoners. He was decorated after the war by the Polish and Czech governments. Shortly after coming to Canada he was also proposed for the French Legion of Honor for his part in saving the lives of French prisoners. The Canadian government, however, refused to allow him to accept the honor, despite its importance to him. "There was some regulation about Canadian citizens not receiving foreign decorations," he explained. "I was very depressed when the word came from Ottawa." So was I when I heard this tale of bureaucratic pettiness.

Witek, whose health had recently begun to deteriorate from the effects of injuries received in the camps long ago, had missed the deadline for applying for restitution from the German government.

"These people are not like you and me," said Dr. Stahr. "They suffer chronic depressions and are forever taking Valium pills. Sometimes they go home and just sit in their rooms for days, not talking or seeing anyone. Some can't keep a job for a week. I have a friend who, when he goes to the movies, will only sit in the last row, with nobody behind him. He is afraid someone will hit him from behind. He cannot go near a dog because he saw people killed by dogs in the camps.

"Some can hardly keep a family. Their marriages break up. One woman used to make her living as a sewing machine operator. She lost an eye when she was beaten with a gun butt, and lately her other eye has gotten weaker. She can't sew well and keeps losing jobs. Her claim lists her as 30 percent disabled, but in effect it is 100 percent because she can no longer support herself. Where is the justice in this?"

Where indeed, I asked myself. I interviewed several more former prisoners, some of whose stories reduced me literally to tears, not only of sadness but of anger that those who had suffered so much should be so harassed later by petty bureaucrats and narrow regulations. The shabby treatment of these people was harder to accept, in many ways, than the official reluctance by Western governments to prosecute the fugitive war criminals within their borders.

The latter failure was partly the result of the legal complexities involved and partly of sheer apathy, as further interviews revealed.

According to an Immigration Department spokesman, even war criminals whose guilt had been established beyond doubt could not be deported from Canada. "No Canadian citizen can be deported to another country," he said. "It is extremely difficult even to deport a noncitizen who has been here five years or more and established domicile. You would have to revoke a person's citizenship first before he could be deported, and I don't think that's ever been done."

If an immigrant gave false information at the time he applied for citizenship, there might be grounds for court action to revoke his citizenship, but "an extremely complex legal procedure would be involved and it's never been tried." The only other way to remove a war criminal, a Justice Ministry spokesman added, would be if a foreign country charged a Canadian citizen with a crime and requested his extradition. Unfortunately, only certain crimes are extraditable offenses—and Canada "does not have extradition treaties with all countries," he added. Hungary, as an example, did not allow its citizens to be extradited to Canada, and under the terms of the law it worked both ways. A recent Canadian request to extradite a Hungarian wanted for murder in Canada was refused by Budapest, he said, and any war criminal wanted by Hungary would not be deported from Canada either.

According to Simon Wiesenthal's Toronto agent, an effort to solve the problem of whether or not persons accused by nations behind the Iron Curtain were guilty of war crimes was mounted in 1963, when then Minister of External Affairs Paul Martin was approached by Jewish groups in Canada. The Soviet government had offered to fly witnesses to Canada, where a special commission similar to the Nuremberg war crimes tribunal would be set up to try the accused according to Canadian judicial standards.

The government was on the verge of accepting the Soviet proposal when it was succeeded by the administration of Prime Minister Pierre

Trudeau. The new Trudeau government let the matter drop. Telephoned in London, England, where he was serving as Canada's High Commissioner to Great Britain, Martin confirmed the essentials of the story. Ottawa had had an opportunity to see justice done but had blown it.

Value Debatable

By this time it seemed unlikely that I would be able to locate more than the fifty-odd alleged war criminals whose names were already on my list, and the value of continuing the hunt for still smaller fry who might be hiding in Canada was debatable. I sat down and wrote the story, the edited version of which ran as a two-part series, one on the war criminals and one on their victims.

The series reported that at least fifty accused or convicted criminals were living peacefully in Canada, where they would probably never be disturbed, while their victims, living side by side with them, continued to suffer and be ignored by the governments directly or indirectly responsible for their plight. The cases of Finta and Kupiak were discussed at length and the legal problems explained.

I was unable to report the discovery of any "big name" criminals-in-hiding, of an Eichmann or a Bormann, and as a spectacular manhunt the story was thus not a success. The series, however, had brought the condition of the former camp victims into public view for the first time, forcing readers to look at an aspect of the war crimes question that had been swept under the rug.

It also stressed Aba Beer's "warning to the living" that the kind of mass killing eventually indulged in by Nazi Germany began on a small scale. It actually began in Germany's hospitals, where the handicapped and the mentally ill—described as "useless eaters" by Karl Binding and Alfred Hoche in their prewar book *The Release of the Destruction of Life Devoid of Value*—were systematically slaughtered.

"I get nervous when I hear anybody talk about eliminating people, about eliminating any class of persons," said Beer. "If somebody says: 'The world would be a paradise without them' that to me is the essence of Hitler's National Socialism. Anybody could be 'them.' Anybody could be a Jew."

The stories also led to a follow-up article, an interview with author/Nazi hunter Beate Klarsfeld, who came to Montreal to promote her book *Wherever They May Be.* "I am proud to be German," said Klarsfeld, who was not herself a Jew. "But our past demands a moral involvement, a change in mentality. Our failure would be an example that would leave the door open to every other fascism in the world." What she said held true not only for Germany, but for everyone.

Chapter X

PORN PROFITS

Obscenity laws in Canada tend to be stricter than those in the United States, which may account for the fact that the booming U.S. pornography industry was slow in establishing itself on the northern side of the American/Canadian border. The porno shops, massage parlors, and peep shows that by the mid-1970's had blighted such places as New York's Times Square and Hollywood's Sunset Strip were only beginning to establish a foothold in Canadian cities when the American public began reacting against them.

Montreal didn't get its first "sex boutique" until 1971, when one place opened its doors on Crescent Street, hub of the city's restaurant and tourist trade.

The heavy coverage of the pornography problem by U.S. papers in 1976 sparked my interest in the subject, and I decided to investigate the status of the industry in Quebec for the Montreal *Gazette*. Working alternately as an editorial writer and temporary assignment editor for the paper, I was forced to conduct the investigation after hours, on my own time. It went slowly, with many interruptions, but in the end proved a worthwhile exercise.

The resulting article showed that pornography—far from being the "harmless outlet" its distributors claim it to be—is a grubby, degrading business and one of the chief financial props of the organized crime syndicates that bleed the North American economy of millions of dollars every year. Although at the time the psychiatric community was divided on the subject, background reading revealed that there were many, including feminist author Susan Brownmiller in *Against Our Wills*, who believed pornography could provoke would-be rapists to action, rather than calm them as other researchers asserted.

The article was also able to demonstrate that on the local level profits from porn had introduced a new element of corruption into the city's law enforcement system and perhaps had paved the way for the invasion of legitimate publishing businesses by organized crime figures.

Subject Ignored

A search of the newspaper's clip files, which included articles culled from all seven of Montreal's French- and English-language daily papers, showed that the subject had been virtually ignored by the press. An English paper had published a single, tongue-in-cheek feature story on the city's first sex boutique (the one on Crescent Street) at the time the shop opened, but that was all. The reporter, a woman who had obviously *not* read Susan Brownmiller, took great delight in making puns about aphrodisiac perfumes and the shop's weird paraphernalia, but made no attempt to address the subject seriously.

A subsequent check of the telephone book and a glance through the display and classified ads in several local tabloid papers, however, revealed that the industry was no joke. On the contrary, it was a booming business. Where there had been only one sex boutique in Montreal in 1971, by 1976 there were more than twenty, most of them concentrated in the tourist and entertainment districts.

The growth in the number of movie theaters devoted exclusively to porn films had shown a similar startling burst of energy. Yet no newspaper had noticed the phenomenon or considered it worth examining.

Who owned the shops, who supplied them, what they sold, and where the profits went struck me as fascinating questions, the answers to which would make interesting reading. As every newsman or woman knows, the words "sex" or "organized crime" in a headline will grab a reader's attention almost automatically. The porn industry's ties to organized crime in the U.S. were already known, and the likelihood was high that the Canadian industry's patterns would parallel their U.S. counterparts. Here, then, was an opportunity to put both of the traditional reader "grabbers" in the same headline while documenting a brand-new phenomenon. Green lights lit. The chase was on.

The first task was to assemble a comprehensive list of the names and locations of each porn shop and skin-flick theater and to find out who owned them. The next step would be to find out what they were selling, for how much, and where the profits went.

Finding the shops' names and addresses was relatively easy. Most of them advertised in the papers, and the appropriate information had only to be copied from the ads. Ownership, however, was another problem. The Quebec Department of Financial Institutions, part of the provincial government, kept track of business ownerships, but there would be no guarantee that the names listed there were not mere fronts for "silent partners" who remained anonymous.

A practical logistics problem was also posed by the fact that a government clerk suddenly asked to look up all the records on nearly fifty businesses (both porn shops and theaters) might balk. The cooperative impulse of the average bureaucrat would likely evaporate at the prospect of spending so much time away from the coffee machine.

To avoid the logistics problem, I decided to make requests for ownership information in batches of five shops or theaters at a time. To solve the silent partner problem, I hoped to be able to quiz police vice squad officers and the owners of rival porn shops, as well as to cross-check names on the government's list with selected Dun and Bradstreet reports.

Accordingly, a request for ownership information on the first five shops was telexed to the Department of Financial Institutions.

While waiting for a response, I used the time to do some further reading on the subject and to contact the Montreal Urban Community (MUC) Police Morality Squad for background information and leads. I also telephoned the Metropolitan Toronto Police "Porn Probe" squad, the vice squads in New York City and Los Angeles, and a Toronto Roman Catholic priest who was attempting to coordinate local church anti-obscenity efforts.

The priest and a detective at Porn Probe provided valuable detail on the industry in Ontario and suggested several good articles on pornography. Doug Payne's "The Shy Pornographers," which appeared in *MacLean's Magazine* on May 3, 1976, and Edward P. Whelan's "Reuben Sturman and his Amazing Porno Empire," in the May 1976 issue of *Cleveland Magazine* proved particularly useful. So did a series of articles in the New York *Times,* written in October 1975 by Nicholas Gage.

To my surprise, the Montreal Police at first proved almost totally useless. The Morality Squad captain initially contacted refused any cooperation, going so far as to make the amazing remark that "whoever owns the porn shops here is none of our [police] business." If it wasn't the Morality Squad's business, I wondered whose it was.

After some persistent badgering, an interview was arranged with a second MUC Morality Squad detective, who had recently made a major prostitution arrest and was said to be familiar also with the porn scene. If he was, he kept it a secret. In an incredibly evasive conversation, he confined himself to displaying several skin magazines the squad had confiscated in earlier raids and stating his belief that the pornography business had no ties to organized crime.

I was amazed, not at the magazines, which were pretty standard smut, but at the detective. I concluded that he was either sadly uninformed about his own specialty or else shy of talking to the press. Perhaps he was involved in some new investigation and didn't want some nosy reporter poking around to blow it, or perhaps he just didn't have time for more question sessions and wanted to brush off his inquisitor. Whatever the reason, I decided for the time being not to waste further efforts on the MUC Police.

(Later, however, I was introduced to another officer who turned out to be a key source. His expertise and cooperation dispelled some of my previous suspicions that the MUC force didn't take its job seriously or that its members were on the take. Some of them, as it turned out, were badly compromised, but not this officer. He cared, and if anyone had tried to bribe him he would have broken the would-be briber's arms.)

Police in New York and Los Angeles, as well as Toronto, were considerably more helpful. They were willing to spend hours on the telephone and to provide written documentation, including carefully constructed charts of ownership interlocks showing how criminals controlled the porn business.

Most printed pornography at the time was being manufactured in three U.S. cities: New York, Los Angeles, and Cleveland. Virtually all of its manufacturers had strong ties to—or actually were—organized crime figures. The same crime connections were found among the wholesale distributors who handled their products.

For example, one of the larger publishers of porn novels and paperbacks was a New York publishing company whose vice-president was listed by the U.S. Justice Department as a member of the Sam DeCavalcante Mafia family of New Jersey. Police said that the Colombo Mafia family also had an interest in the company's various enterprises.

Another major firm was controlled by a Cleveland man whose company formed the nucleus of a worldwide pornography empire. He was apparently not an actual "Made Man" member of the Mafia, but police said he had ties to mob-backed operations from Boston to Los Angeles. His own business records showed he paid one-third of his net monthly profits from a news agency in Boston to a well-known Massachusetts mob figure.

Telltale Names

Armed with a list of such names, I began touring the local porn shops to see what they had on their shelves. In virtually every store I found books and magazines with the same telltale names on their inside covers.

At each shop I bought samples of the merchandise, demanding a sales slip as proof of the place of purchase. The demand for a sales slip astonished several of the store clerks, whose usual customers were so furtive and anxious to get out of the store unseen that they didn't bother about such things. For me, however, the sales slips were essential. With them and the actual merchandise in hand I could back up a published statement that such-and-such a store was selling books produced by firms dominated by organized crime. On the outside of each plain brown wrapper I wrote the date and time of purchase.

By this time, reports were starting to come back from the Department of Financial Institutions listing the owners of the various shops. Each batch of names was duly cross-checked with the names in the newspaper's clipping files, but none of them had been mentioned in the paper before. They were ingenues, waiting to be discovered.

My police contacts also checked the criminal records and found that, except for a scattering of local arrests on obscenity charges, the owners' records were clean. Usually the obscenity conviction involved no more than the payment of a modest fine and confiscation of the offending literature. This relative lack of serious criminal records was disappointing, but the investigation was only beginning.

Up to this point, none of the porn shop owners knew they were being scrutinized by a reporter, and I decided that it was time to introduce myself.

I started at the bottom, with the sales clerks in the stores, informing them that I was doing "a feature on the whole sex shop phenomenon" and asking the kind of questions someone interested only in a "color" story would ask: What kind of people come in here as customers? Do they seem embarrassed? How did you get into this job? Does the owner give you a decent salary or is he a miser? What is your personal opinion of pornography? Do you read these books yourself?

They were the kind of queries that might have been asked by the reporter who wrote the "cutesy" feature on Montreal's first sex boutique. Essentially it was pure drivel, but I knew these conversations would be reported to the stores' owners and wanted them to consider me a potential source of good publicity, rather than a possible troublemaker.

The approach paid off. The shop owners took the bait, and before long I was setting up interviews with them. One owner telephoned personally to request an interview, noting that he was about to open a new branch store and that an article now would be a boon to business. Photo possibilities, he added, were excellent. He was full of enthusiasm.

While the interviews were being scheduled, regular rubbish pickups were proceeding at each shop, and the *Gazette's* comptroller had obtained Dun and Bradstreet reports on some of the publishers and wholesale distributors whose names had turned up among the local boutiques' stock. Unlike the people at the retail level, whose records were fairly clean, the wholesale and publishing people with whom they dealt often had long arrest records. Some had been involved in fraudulent bankruptcies, a traditional mob money-maker, and others were well known to police in New York and Los Angeles as organized crime hangers-on.

Although the Montreal police had not been particularly helpful thus far, one Morality Squad officer had supplied a valuable tidbit of information that the co-owner of one of the city's sex shops was a former civilian employee of the police department who had actually worked for the Morality Squad itself. "Working here must have given him ideas," the policeman had quipped.

By coincidence, this idea man was the same owner who had called to request an interview to publicize his new store, and I decided to start the interviews with him and his partner. It seemed a fruitful avenue to pursue but turned out to be even more fruitful than expected.

The two partners were brothers, both ambitious businessmen, and the brother who had worked for the police was a compulsive talker. We met in a cramped office piled with bills, invoices, and cartons of merchandise, tucked behind what he called "the most successful sex boutique in Montreal." The contrast between the crowded, dusty office and the luxurious showroom was striking.

Whether the shop really was successful I couldn't yet judge, but it certainly was bizarre. On the shelves, between rubber mannequins dressed in frilly lingerie, were a crazy assortment of vibrators and rubber toys. Soothing Musak played over an unseen loudspeaker while customers—all male—thumbed with intense concentration through the skin magazines and pulp novels on the book racks. An effeminate sales clerk floated from customer to customer, making small talk and—apparently without much success—trying to pry them away from the magazines and toward the cash register. The clerk, like the customers, was male, breaking the pattern of other such shops where the sales staff were mostly women and mostly with plunging necklines.

The shop owner, who also acted as a wholesaler for several other local boutiques, was so eager for publicity that the interview almost conducted itself. We talked for nearly an hour, philosophizing on the changing mores of society, on the alleged therapeutic values of porn for repressed personalities, the whole shot.

Then, in what appeared to be a casual aside, I asked about the owner's former job at the MUC Police Morality Squad. I laughed, dropping the question as a half-joking comment. His reply was a bombshell:

"That's my brother you're talking about," he said. "But if you think that's a coincidence, one of the shops here is actually owned by a policeman . . ."

"A policeman?" I asked, heart thumping. "Who?"

He told me the name, adding: "Don't tell him I told you. He's a competitor, you know. I don't want the Morality Squad down here raiding me every other day."

This was the kind of classic break that gladdens the soul of every investigator. Heart still thumping, I quickly changed the subject, talked a bit more, and then ended the interview. Now the story was really shaping up!

I took a cab back to the office and, sure enough, there, on the latest owners' list from the Department of Financial Institutions, was the name of the policeman. He was "secretary/treasurer" of a chain of sex shops that had recently made a wholesaling agreement with a second chain. The resulting group was the second largest in the city, rivaled only by the chain owned by the man I had just interviewed.

A call to the MUC Police Personnel Division located the station where the officer was assigned and confirmed that he was indeed an active-duty officer. This was paydirt enough for my effort, but there was more. The policeman's shops had actually been raided once by MUC Police and a quantity of legally obscene material confiscated. The shop and the policeman's brother (a co-owner) had been cited and convicted on obscenity charges, but the officer himself had not been convicted.

Enough to Print

Much work remained to be done on the porn film industry in the city and province, but as far as the book and magazine outlets were concerned I now had enough to print an initial story. I had confirmed that Montreal's sex shops were a booming business, that they sold retail merchandise supplied by wholesalers with criminal records and manufactured by companies controlled by organized crime. The co-owner of one group of shops was a former civilian employee of the police, and another chain was part-owned by a police officer. The officer's ownership was a blatant conflict of interest, as he was sworn as a lawman to uphold the very statutes his shop had been convicted of violating.

It was time to clinch this part of the story. I telephoned the policeman at his station just as his shift was getting off work and hit him by surprise. He admitted everything, insisting only that he had recently sold his interest in the shops "to my brother."

Further checking showed that a departmental inquiry had been held after the raid on his shops and the officer had been ordered by his superiors to sell his interest in the business. There was no record yet of an actual sale having been made. The policeman had not been convicted on the obscenity charge, a department public relations spokesman explained, because the presiding judge had ruled that the obscene material seized "may have been purchased without his knowledge."

I wrote the story the same day, and the newspaper's lawyer looked it over that night. He warned that we should make absolutely certain that the officer had indeed sold his interest in the shops and suggested the precise wording we should use to describe the incident without leaving ourselves open to a libel charge. One of the lawyer's own staff went to the provincial capital at Quebec City and checked the most recent business records, discovering that the officer had been truthful. His shares had, in fact, been sold to his brother only a week or two earlier.

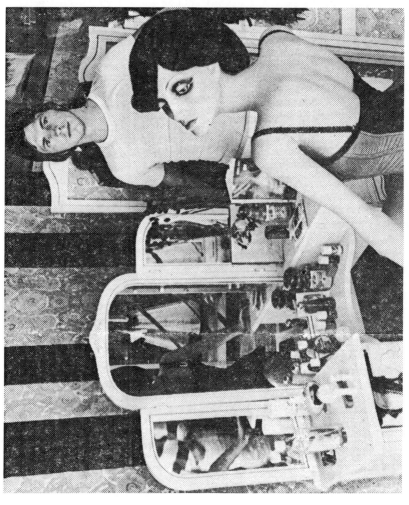

The involvement of a Montreal police officer and persons linked to organized crime in the profitable pornography business was outlined in this 1977 story. Pornography is a major source of revenue for the Mafia.

The story, carefully worded and accompanied by a note to the copy desk, was left in the copy box to be published while I went away on vacation. The note accompanying the story stressed that the paragraph wording suggested by the paper's lawyer should not be changed.

The reliability of the desk, in this case, turned out to be dismal. The story, which ran July 18, 1977, appeared with only one section reworded: precisely the one the lawyer had requested us not to change. As the story appeared in the paper, we were wide open to a libel charge.

Naturally, I was furious at this, especially as a note had been left with the copy warning against tampering, but fortunately the policeman never sued. The story was subsequently picked up by the French-language papers, and Montreal readers, both French and English, got their first real glimpse of what the pornography industry in their city was all about.

As the article reported, the business was extremely profitable. A skin magazine that could be purchased wholesale in the U.S. for a dollar might be sold retail in Montreal for as much as $7.50 to $20, depending on whether it was a mildly soft-core—and hence legal—magazine showing only nudes, or a hard-core bit of perversion sold under the counter.

The retailer and wholesaler usually split profits 60/40, a part of it going back eventually to what one Toronto policeman termed "the pocket of some Mafia don in the States."

Unfortunately I was never able to follow up the initial story with an investigation of the porn film industry in Quebec or the links I found between a major wholesale periodical distributor in the province and U.S. organized crime interests. The *Gazette* ordered me to cease making inquiries. One editor told me that, even if the Quebec distributor was really controlled by a New Jersey crime family (as I suggested) the readers would not be interested. Reporting that the Mafia might actually control what was or was not sold on newsstands in the province would not tell readers "anything useful," he said.

The key elements of this investigation turned out to be the backgrounding phase, where the organized crime links of the pornography publishers and distributors were discovered, and the interview with the sex shop owner who revealed his rival's dual function as a police officer.

The chief weakness of the effort was the lack of follow-up and my own failure to keep an eye on the copy as it went through the desk, the print shop, and into the paper. It should never have been left behind—note or no note—when I went on vacation. Only pure luck stood between this oversight and a lost libel action.

Chapter XI

MISCELLANY

Some stories, like the hunt for hidden Nazis, drag on for months, taxing the patience of both the reporter and his editors. Others may reach a successful conclusion—or a dead end—in days or even hours. Every case is unique and each one, even those that end in failure, teaches the reporter some new lesson or trick of the trade, adding to the depth of his or her experience.

One of the most valuable experiences I can recall was a 24-hour period spent on the street in a quiet Michigan university town in 1969, tracing the recent movements of a student via the campus grapevine. It was a concentrated series of high-pressure lessons in both interview technique and the art of tracking missing persons, a short course that resulted in several national beats (the first stories in print on an event of national interest) for the Detroit *News.*

It began with a routine feature assignment from the *News'* suburban bureau, a request to do a series of interviews with two Wayne County Sheriff's Department policewomen and write a report on "a typical day in the life of a policewoman." The story turned out to be anything but typical.

I ended up making friends with the two women, and both were pleased with the initial draft of the story. This was fortunate. Neither officer mentioned it during the earlier interviews, but they were working on a major mass-murder investigation involving the killing of several female students at a nearby university. As I was riding in the squad car with them one morning, a call came in on the radio asking them to help pick up a suspect.

It was the mass murderer. "We're about to arrest the co-ed killer; want to come along?" one policewoman asked. Obviously, I did. The story had been on page one for months and had drawn national attention to the tree-shaded college town where the killings had taken place. If this was to be the climax of the police pursuit, it would be a great story.

The actual arrest was as climactic as expected. The suspect, head hanging, was led away in handcuffs. His roommate attacked my photographer, trying to throw him down a stairwell. Quotes and inside informa-

112

Can't be co-ed killer, friends say

Suspect an 'All-American boy'

John Norman Collins, accused of murdering one girl and being investigated in six other slayings involving torture and sexual sadism, is the living, breathing embodiment of the All-American boy.

"He was a really nice guy — the kind you would let your sister go out with," said Ken Roe, of Pittsfield Village, a former student at Eastern Michigan University who worked with Collins last year in the university's alumni office.

After the 22-year-old Collins was arrested yesterday and charged w i t h the first-degree murder of Karen Sue Beineman, an 18-year-old EMU freshman, a team of Detroit News

The arrest of a 22-year-old Eastern Michigan University senior from Center Line for the murder of an EMU coed the latest victim in seven such Washtenaw County murders, caught everyone by surprise. To find out what the suspect was like, The Detroit News sent four reporters — Thomas F. Pawlick Suzanne Hemmen, Al Stark and Nancy Abner to question those who knew him. Here, written by Robert A. Popa, is their report.

reporters interviewed dozens of persons who know him.

What emerged from their interviews was a picture of a youth who is outwardly well-adjusted, popular both with girls and men, respectful of his mother, accomplished as an athlete and motorcycle rider, neat in appear-

ance and the way he kept his personal belongings, and a good student.

NONE OF THOSE interviewed could believe Collins is capable of one murder let alone several.

Even the Theta Chi fraternity brothers who expelled Collins last year for nonpayment of Center Line, has medium-long hair with fashionable, earlobe length sideburns. He is clean-shaven and usually described as a neat dresser.

Collins, whose home address is 7327 Helen, dues had remained friendly with him.

At St. Clement Roman Catholic High School in Center Line, Collins s h a r e d the football team's captaincy with two others. He was an offensive end and safetyman who was awarded letters as a sophomore, junior and senior.

Said the high school's 1965 yearbook, "Crest":

"Collins, sparkling end for the green and gold, has been a letterman since his sophomore year. His fine blocking has resulted in many extra yards for Crusader ball-carriers.

"Leading the way, he pokes holes in op-

posing lines, smashing through to open the field for the touchdown.

"Collins pokes holes in other things besides the opposing football lines, as any of his classmates will tell you. An alert debater, he is a ready participant in class discussions, where instead of an opposing lineman, another student's argument is his target.

"Naturally curious, Collins digs through to something until he is satisfied."

AFTER GRADUATION, Collins attended Central Michigan University in Mt. Pleasant. He entered in September, 1965, and left in June, 1966, after completing his freshman year.

Officials at Central Michigan say Collins was a good pupil, that he stayed out of trouble and that he left of his own choosing.

While at Central, Collins lived in Barnard Hall, a men's dormitory.

Transferring to Eastern Michigan in September, 1966, Collins joined Theta Chi fraternity and moved into the fraternity house on West Cross Street just across from Eastern's music department building.

Wayne Patterson, a fraternity brother from Toledo, said Collins was expelled from the fraternity "about a year ago" for nonpayment of the $40-a-semester dues and for nonattendance at meetings.

113

Tracking the movements of a mass murderer via the campus grapevine was essential to the task.

tion were flying back and forth. It was all great, dramatic stuff. But the best information came last.

"You know, this wasn't the only kid involved," one of the policewomen told me later. "There's a whole bunch of them we've been watching. In a way, I'm sorry they had to make the bust on this guy now, because we haven't got enough on the others yet." It was a bombshell, but the two officers wouldn't add anything to this cryptic remark. When I telephoned the paper to dictate the arrest story, I told the assistant managing editor about the possibility that a group of students might be involved.

"Don't come in," he said. "Stay out there and dig up every damn detail you can." For the next day and night I did just that. My method was to go from student to student, from group to group, sometimes openly identifying myself as a reporter, sometimes posing as a mere casual bystander, listening, probing, eavesdropping, and questioning. I was looking for any information at all on either the arrested student or his friends, including the latter's names and addresses.

Bringing up the subject of the arrest was easy. The papers and TV news programs were full of the case, and everyone was talking about it. The town was buzzing, alive with rumors and speculation. I returned several times to a diner near the house where the suspected killer had lived and listened to the neighbors gossip. The jackpot rang when a fraternity brother of the young man turned up and showed no reluctance to discuss the case with a friendly stranger at the lunch counter.

He gave me the names of several other students who knew the suspect, and they in turn gave me other names. The trail led from person to person, interview to interview, and finished with one of the prisoner's two best friends. The first was his roommate, already mentioned, whom other students described as "a real goo-goo, all screwed up." The second friend was "goo-goo" too, but in a different, more sinister way.

The photographer and I met him in his attic room in one of the big frame houses that lined the streets in the older residential section of the town. He smiled an odd, mocking smile when we entered the room, and as we talked he sat holding a black cat on his lap and stroking its back over and over again. His eyes were hard. Asked if he thought his friend had committed all of the murders, he smiled an even more mocking smile and answered: "No, I don't think he did."

Later, leaving the house, the photographer admitted: "That guy was weird. He really gave me the creeps." Shortly after the interview, the friend left town, moving to California.

Other police officers to whom I subsequently talked agreed with the policewomen, telling me they were convinced the arrested student— who was later convicted of murder and sentenced to life imprisonment—

was not alone in committing his crimes. I thought of this a couple of years afterward, when a similar rash of killings broke out in another part of the country. They followed the same pattern as the Michigan murders, in uncanny detail. The state where they took place was California.

I took out the old clips from the *News* to look at them again when this new series of killings began and was struck by the composite drawings that had been published with one *News* article. They were sketches a police artist had put together from the descriptions of witnesses and were remarkably similar, not to the photos of the arrested student, but to those of his friend with the black cat. (The friend's yearbook photo had also been printed in the papers.)

The information gathered in those frenetic interviews after the arrest had turned up enough detail to keep the *News'* coverage of the story ahead of everyone else's, but they also taught me much about the value of the grapevine and the almost compulsive urge to talk of people who suddenly find themselves close to a major news story. Even the friend, who may well have been involved in the murders, couldn't stop himself from talking. Sitting there, stroking his black cat, he *had* to speak. A week earlier or a week later, before or after the peak of excitement marked by the arrest, he would no doubt have remained closemouthed, but at that precise moment in the drama he talked. My own skill as an interviewer was not well developed at the time, but a policeman experienced at questioning might have gotten a confession that day. Maybe someday another policeman will obtain one, and the Michigan murders will really be solved.

The technique of plugging into a grapevine and following it along, like an electrician following a colored wire, proved itself in several investigations. It tends to be most valuable in small or close-knit communities, such as a university campus or a small town. Only a few months after the Michigan murder case, I was assigned to fly to Berkeley, California, to look up Mario Savio, originator of the celebrated 1960's quote "Don't trust anyone over thirty." Savio, for personal reasons, had withdrawn from public life and did not want to talk to newsmen, but the grapevine helped me track him down. I got the interview.

Wild Rice

Time can be a prominent factor in many inquiries, as evidenced in an investigation conducted for *Harrowsmith Magazine* in early 1979.

The story began with a free-lance submission from a woman in northern Ontario, a writer who lived on the Sabaskong Indian Reserve near the legendary Lake of the Woods. The free-lancer, Kathi Avery, was

Last Stand In Wild Rice Country

*"You cannot take from us
what Manitou has given," say the Ojibway.
"Just watch us," say their white competitors.*

By Kathi Avery and Thomas Pawlick

Illustrations by Wayne Yerxa

Each summer for more than a thousand years, a man like Shuniah Goneb has stood alone on the shores of Sabaskong Bay in the Lake of the Woods watershed, looking with anticipation across the quiet water to where the brown and green seeds of *manoomin* ripen in the August sun.

The Ojibway patriarch, now in his 68th year, is short and stocky of build, his body worn and rounded like a great boulder in a river. His once jet-black hair has turned white and there are heavy crinkles around his eyes. He is an old man, but the task before him fills him with quiet excitement and satisfaction, the kind that makes him feel young again. He is about to initiate his people's annual wild rice harvest.

No one knows what name Shuniah Goneb's prehistoric forebears, those whom modern archaeologists call the Laurel Culture, gave to the long-stemmed plants, swaying gently four to eight feet above the water's surface. But the Ojibway descendants speak sometimes of *Manitou gi ti gahn*, "the plant the Great Spirit gave us," but more often the bands of today call it *manomin* — from *Manitou*, meaning Great Spirit and *meenun*, meaning delicacy.

It is a sacred plant, as central to the ancient Ojibway religion as bread and wine to Christians, but it is a staple, too, a food that can be stored for years (the ancients created dry stone-lined caches hidden along the shores of their lakes and rivers) and that could fill the hungry interstices of a hunting and fishing society.

Shuniah Goneb has been chosen by the Sabaskong elders at Crow Portage to conduct the annual pre-harvest ritual of gathering a handful of grain from each of the bays where the band's families will pick their crop. When the elder returns, the wild rice will be boiled in a pot and divided among all the rice harvesters. Like a Christian communion, it is both a solemn event and the occasion for a celebration. In the old days, Shuniah Goneb recalls, "The old men used to sing and we'd dance all night. It wasn't the kind of tourist-pow-wow you see today, with costumed dancers fancy-stepping around the

116

An attempt to move in on the profitable wild rice market put some entrepreneurs and government officials in a potential conflict-of-interest situation. The Indians' fight to keep control of the resource was outlined in this Harrowsmith article.

an idealistic young woman deeply shocked by the social and economic problems burdening Canada's native peoples, especially those in the Lake of the Woods region.

Already poverty-stricken by the standards of the majority culture, the Ojibway there had recently sustained a crippling economic blow when deadly mercury pollution from nearby paper mills was found in the English/Wabigoon River system. The government shut down many local tourist and fishing lodges and warned the Indians not to eat fish caught in the area. Thus not only did the Ojibway lose a staple food from their diet, but many Indians who had worked as guides for sport fishermen were thrown out of work.

Not long after this reverse, still another attack was mounted on the Indians' fragile economic base. Lured by the high prices wild rice was bringing on the gourmet foods market, white entrepreneurs launched an effort to wrest the exclusive right to harvest wild rice on Indian land away from the Ojibway, who had been guaranteed control of the harvest in earlier treaties. One of the leaders of this takeover attempt, Avery wrote, was the campaign manager and political right-hand man of a prominent provincial cabinet minister, whose past and present responsibilities were closely intertwined with management of the rice resource. It was a classic conflict of interest.

Unfortunately Avery, despite her familiarity with the story and the considerable in-depth research she had done, had little investigative experience and only a rough idea of how to document the conflict so as to avoid libel difficulties. The magazine handed the latter task over to me.

I decided to fly to Kenora, Ontario, to work directly with Avery rather than attempt to deal with the subject by telephone, but I knew I had only a limited budget—and hence limited time—to get the job done. At most, I could afford to spend four or five days on the scene. Any additional work would have to be done via long-distance phone.

To make the best use of the time that would be available, I spent two days at the office reading all of Avery's material and making a detailed list of questions that still needed answering. I also drew up an outline of possible sources of information, listed in order of importance and "spookability." By the time the Norontair Twin Otter bumped to a landing in Kenora one cold morning in February, my itinerary had already been blocked out. A quick introductory lunch with Avery in a local restaurant, and we were out on the street, knocking on doors.

We covered every local source of documentation, plus several personal interviews with participants in the story, in three days. Given the complexity of the story, I was tempted to submit this feat to the *Guinness Book of Records* but didn't know under which category to enter it! We weren't able to meet the "Rule of Two Sources" test on every question, but we did manage to back up nearly every important point with at least one document or quote. Any proof still lacking after my trip could be gathered from the home office of *Harrowsmith.*

Our rounds included two visits to the Kenora office of the federal Department of Indian Affairs, two to the district office of the Ontario Ministry of Natural Resources, three trips to the local Land Registry Office, four to the office of the Treaty Three Organization (grouping the various Indian tribes that were parties to the original treaty covering rice rights), two to the local newspaper, the *Kenora Daily Miner and News,* plus personal interviews with ten or more people linked in some way with the story. In the evenings, when government offices were closed and document searches curtailed, I sat in the hotel restaurant poring over what we had turned up with Avery, her husband, and a local attorney who supported the Ojibway cause.

Much of what we found was simply backup to what Avery had written. For example, she had called a wild rice entrepreneur a "political crony" of the Minister of Northern Affairs. A visit to the *Daily Miner and News* office turned up several newspaper clippings from earlier political campaigns in which the entrepreneur was quoted at length and referred to as the minister's "campaign manager." A photo of the two together, celebrating the minister's victory in the last election, was printed on page one of a postelection edition. We obtained a copy of the original photo. Later, writing from *Harrowsmith's* office, I obtained from the government copies of the campaign expense records listing contributors' names.

The Indians claimed they had established rights to harvest wild rice on their own territory. In Kenora, we located an actual copy of the original, handwritten version of Treaty Three, signed and witnessed by two half-breed interpreters a century before, in which those rights were outlined. The official, printed version of that ancient treaty circulated by the Department of Indian Affairs differed from the original on several key points. It was obvious that the government had altered the terms of the original treaty, a fact that we pointed out in our subsequent article.

Avery's original story charged that the white campaign manager was being "favored" by the government over the local Ojibway when it came to helping develop a wild rice industry. Our visits to the Land Registry Office allowed us to document this. While Indian requests for government help were delayed or refused, the white campaign manager was obtaining $182,000 in government development loans, some interest-free, to help develop his rice company. Because they were mortgage loans, secured by his land as collateral, they were recorded along with the other information at the deeds office.

Avery's story had charged that the campaign manager was trying to take over control of all of the rice-producing areas in northern Ontario. In Kenora, we obtained maps from the Ministry of Natural Resources showing the locations of the rice-producing lakes. Later I obtained an official list from the MNR of all those who held permits to harvest rice on those lakes. In case the list was not complete, I also telephoned every MNR district office in the rice-growing region and asked each MNR officer if the minister's friend had any rice-harvesting licenses in that jurisdiction. The campaign manager turned out to hold the lion's share of rice-harvesting permits in northern Ontario.

In the end, we managed to amass so much documentation during my brief trip north (and through subsequent follow-up phone calls) that it required a second, sidebar story in addition to the main article on wild rice to describe it all to the readers.

Sandwiching so much fact-gathering into a few days wasn't the only aspect of the story where timing was important, however. The indispensable interviews with the minister and his "political crony," as well as with a few key supporting actors in the drama, also had to be timed correctly.

For example, a check of *Scott's Industrial Directory* revealed the names of the officers of the campaign manager's rice company. A search of each of these officers' backgrounds showed that the firm's advertising and public relations director was also an employee of the government department over which the minister in question presided. Obviously, we needed this man's quotes in his own defense before we could publish anything. Equally obviously, he would be sure to tip the minister if a reporter called him.

On the other hand, if we called the minister or his pal first they would probably warn the public relations director not to talk. Whom to phone first thus became a bit of a problem. I decided to phone the public relations director on the theory that, taken by surprise, he would be much more likely to blurt things out than would his seasoned politician boss. (As it turned out, the decision was not necessary. The public relations man was on vacation outside the province, and I was able to reach him at his hotel. He would not be phoning his boss until he returned to the province.)

As for the minister and his campaign manager, I phoned them both the same day, and, judging from their responses, neither had had a chance to talk to the other before my call.

The way the interviews were conducted was also important, as the approach taken would in part govern whatever actions the two men might take to cover their tracks. I didn't want to alarm them unduly, as some of the documentation I needed was not yet in my hands.

Accordingly, when they answered the telephone I told them that I was an editor "checking out a freelancer's story to see if she has her facts straight." This, of course, was true, but the way the introduction was phrased allowed them to jump to the conclusion that I might be suspicious of the freelancer's reliability. The next logical step would be to assume that they could easily hand me a line, disparage the freelancer, and get the story killed. I did nothing to contradict such a notion should it happen to enter their heads. Both men gave long, detailed interviews and both said goodbye afterwards, convinced that I had been won over to their view.

I hadn't. The subsequent story tore them to shreds.

The Letters Column

As already noted, the follow-up to an article can often make the difference in deciding whether that story will have a measurable impact or be forgotten the day after it appears. Additional stories containing new material are the best kind of follow-up, but the Letters to the Editor column of a newspaper or magazine can also be a valuable tool in reinforcing the original message.

The story on the health consequences of the nuclear accident at Three Mile Island, described in Chapter VIII, was a case in point. The numerous attacks by nuclear industry spokesmen on the magazine and those quoted in it provided us with excuse after excuse to amplify our original message. The more influential the person criticizing the story, the more likely his attack and our reply were to be read by the public and commented upon.

Consequently, we printed nearly every attack—except those that were too long or too obviously false to dignify in print—and followed each letter with an editorial reply of our own. These debates and rebuttals added a whole new dimension to the story. As one reader commented after reading a particularly spirited exchange: "Having read Dr. Arthur Porter's letter, 'Porter Reacts,' and the response from the authors, I think that you have rather effectively shut down at least one reactor (namely Porter)."

A pamphlet attacking the story, written by a government nuclear scientist and circulated by government officials, provided a peg for a three-page editorial defending the "Silent Toll" stories—and introducing new statistical evidence supporting the thesis.

The sequence was similar after *Harrowsmith* published a story exposing the inefficient, unjust, and confusing system through which Bell Canada served its rural telephone customers. The article provoked angry reactions from Bell's public relations staff, as well as from federal Department of Communications bureaucrats. Their reactions were like gifts from heaven.

Both Bell's PR people and a government bureaucrat wrote to correct an error in the story in which an incorrect investment figure had been given. Unfortunately for the letter writers, they had forgotten—or assumed we would ignore—the fact that the figure in question was originally obtained from *them*. The dollar amount quoted in the magazine story was taken from a Bell document and an article written by the government employee. As the editor's reply pointed out (with secret glee): "They are, in effect, writing to correct themselves."

Of course, once on the subject of Bell's wayward activities again, the editor's reply did not fail to add still more details of the company's bungling, details that had been left out of the original story due to lack of space. If it hadn't been for the opportunity provided by the letter writers, these extra details might never have gotten into print.

In many ways, publication of an exposé story is like publication of a scientist's theory in a scientific journal. Just as the scientist is customarily attacked by skeptics and allowed by the journal to reply to these attacks in subsequent issues, so the investigative reporter is bound to be attacked by his critics. The Letters to the Editor column and the editorial reply constitute the equivalent of scientific debate over what he has written, over his "theory" concerning the guilt or innocence of those about whom he writes.

Sometimes the reporter may be interviewed by other media, including radio and television newspeople, about a controversial story. If the format of such an interview includes the presence of an opponent, the reporter must be able to speak as well as he writes. Skill in debate, in both written and verbal riposte, is a worthwhile attribute. Sooner or later it will come in handy.

It is easier to see through spurious arguments and compose a convincing rebuttal if one has a solid grasp of the basic rules of logic and of debate. A familiarity with the standard techniques of political propaganda is also helpful, if only to spot when an opponent is using them.

The rules of logic, of how the old-time Thomistic theologians told the difference between a valid syllogism and an invalid sophism, are outlined in standard textbooks on logic. Any reporter could benefit from reading some of these texts or from taking a course in elementary logic at a local college or university. A good public library should have several such texts on its shelves, listed under philosophy, logic, or perhaps propaganda.

Two books I have personally found useful are *How to Argue,* by David J. Crossley and Peter A. Wilson, and *La Propagande Politique (Political Propaganda),* by J. M. Domenach.

Both the Letters to the Editor column and the treatment given a story by other news media are closely watched by the officials charged with regulating whatever situations the reporter exposes. If no letters appear and other media ignore the story, the officials responsible will ignore the article too. If letters come in but most of them attack the story, the officials will not only do nothing about conditions but will chuckle happily at the journalist's discomfiture.

If, however, the readers' letters support the story, other media begin picking it up, and none of the reporter's critics can prove him wrong, the bureaucrats and politicians will become nervous. It may become impossible for them to pooh-pooh the reporter's revelations. Enough letters and they may even be pressured into doing their jobs.

Another attribute the investigative reporter would do well to cultivate is "brass"—nerve, the ability to bluff.

In one case, the author and a friend were investigating a real estate broker suspected of perpetrating a massive land fraud. To gain evidence that would stand up in a libel trial, we needed access to the broker's rubbish, but his garbage bags were always placed *inside* the back door to his office until the DPW trucks arrived. To make matters worse, the storeroom where the bags were piled was in plain view of one part of the inner office where the realtor and his employees worked.

Getting at those bags without being seen was a knotty problem, but we solved it. My friend, pretending to be a prospective client, went into the office and engaged the staff in conversation. He stood in such a way that those inside, if they paid attention to him, would be looking away from the storeroom.

While he distracted the staff, I ducked inside, snatched the two big plastic bags, and ducked back out. At any point, one of the office staff could have turned and spotted me, giving the game away and also laying us open to charges of trespassing. Fortunately, no one turned.

Photographer Steve Kennedy, with whom the author worked on several stories, had enough nerve for a small army of people, all in one personality. Together, we bluffed our way into mental hospitals, offices, and the confidence of various malefactors. Without brass—the kind of self-assurance that allows its possessor to convince others that he belongs where he is—we would never have gotten into, much less out of, half of the places we went.

One would think that a security guard at a mental hospital, seeing one man with a camera and another with a notepad enter, would be a bit suspicious of their tale that they were visitors there to see a patient-relative. In realty, the guard was not. The men projected such confidence and assurance that, psychologically, it was impossible to suspect them. They gained admittance, camera and all, and not until several days later when a story exposing unsanitary hospital conditions—graphically illustrated with photos—appeared on the front page of the paper did that guard realize who his visitors really were.

An investigator has to be a bit of a con man, to take a leaf from his quarry's book, to get the evidence he needs.

PART THREE

LIMITATIONS

Chapter XII

LIBEL AND SLANDER

According to the *Concise Oxford Dictionary,* to defame is to "attack the good reputation of, or speak ill of" a person or group of persons. Written defamation is referred to as libel; the spoken variety is called slander.

In American and British common law, a statement usually must be false as well as damaging to someone's reputation in order to qualify as an offense. Truth is thus the author's refuge. However, in some European countries and in Canada's Quebec Province (which in part follows the Napoleonic Code rather than British common law), even a true statement can be a defamation if its author had "malicious intent" in publishing or broadcasting it.

Because nearly every story an investigative reporter writes is going to damage the reputation of some person, group, or business, a firm grasp of the principles involved in libel and slander law is absolutely essential to the journalist's survival. So is a knowledge of the more recent "invasion of privacy" statutes and, last but far from least, a feeling for the art of negotiation—the time-honored poker player's knack of bluff and counterbluff.

Many a newspaper has actually committed libel but headed off a suit through astute handling of the injured party. For every libel suit that goes before a judge, a hundred may be settled out of court or fended off by sheer bluff.

The late Drew Pearson, author of the nationally syndicated column "The Washington Merry-Go-Round" and journalistic mentor of Jack Anderson, was a past master at handling libel suit threats. His columns skewering crooked U.S. politicians and incompetent bureaucrats were constantly greeted by choruses of anger and threats to sue.

Few such threats were ever carried out, however, because Pearson always seemed to have more on the injured party than was included in the published column. Threats had a way of vanishing as soon as an irate politician suspected that Pearson might be in a position to reveal still more of his transgressions. Rather than have all of his sins exposed, the pol would decide to do nothing about those that had been revealed so far.

Pearson, of course, documented his allegations thoroughly, and even if one of his targets went ahead with a suit, the chances of the plaintiff's winning were virtually nil.

Proof and Privilege

A libel must have actually been published or a slander actually broadcast before a suit can be launched over it, and the suit must be launched within a specified time limit. In some states and Canadian provinces the injured party has three months after publication in which to file suit, in others a year; but whatever the limit, the right to sue is lost if the plaintiff waits too long to take action.

Once a suit has been launched, the plaintiff may seek damages under three different headings: (1) punitive or exemplary damages, assessed as an outright punishment of the writer or an example to warn other authors; (2) compensatory or special damages, assessed to reimburse the injured party for provable financial losses suffered because of the libel; and (3) nominal damages, assessed when a technical libel has been proven but the degree of injury is slight and no malice was involved.

In general, courts are stricter in libel cases than they are in slander cases, because it is commonly considered easier to make an inadvertent slip of the tongue than of the typewriter. A statement is more likely to have been born of malice if its author had time to deliberate over it than if it was spoken on the spur of the moment.

In most states and provinces the burden of proof in libel cases is on the publisher, who must establish to the judge's satisfaction that whatever was printed was lawful. Unlike most defendants, the writer and publisher are presumed guilty until proven innocent. The means they may employ to defend themselves vary, depending on whether they are dealing with a U.S. or a Canadian court.

In the U.S., a statement may be defended on any of three grounds: (1) *justification,* namely, proof that the statement was true; (2) *privilege,* or proof that the statement was a fair report of a public proceeding by a duly constituted legislative or judicial body; and (3) *fair comment,* that is, that the statement expressed an honest opinion on a matter open to public criticism.

A good guide used by many reporters to insure a defense of justification for themselves is to follow the "Rule of Two Sources." Before publishing any controversial statement, they first make sure that they have two authentic documents, two reliable witnesses, or a document and a witness to cite as sources. If the writer can produce such proof, his story will be practically unassailable in court. Even one source, provided it is absolutely authentic and reliable, will do the job.

If there is no document or witness to support a statement, however, the reporter who publishes it may be in deep trouble. The same holds true if the document cannot be proven genuine, or if a witness is shown to be unreliable (for example, a witness with a prior criminal record including a conviction for fraud or perjury).

It is not enough for a journalist to be morally certain that persons or groups are crooked before calling them such in print. The reporter must be able to *demonstrate* that the story's targets are, in fact, crooks.

As for privilege, reporters are on slightly firmer ground. The transcript of a trial, a quotation from the *Congressional Record* or Canada's *Hansard,* or a direct quote taken down during the course of an official proceeding cannot be assailed as libel as long as the reporter's description of it was straightforward and contained no "personal opinion" or "editorializing."

The theory behind this rule is that legislators and plaintiffs in open court should not be hindered in speaking their minds, and that a fair and impartial rendering of what was said in such a forum is fitting matter for the public to hear. The citizen's right to know what is going on in his legislature or courts is paramount, even if what is said there might not be true.

This does not, of course, excuse the reporter from detailing both sides of a question, or from being fair. Obviously, to recount only what the prosecutor said in a trial, ignoring what defense lawyers said and failing to inform readers that the defendant was found innocent, would not be acceptable.

In Canada, the idea of privilege is interpreted in such a way as to allow reporters much less leeway than is given their U.S. counterparts. One Montreal reporter, for example, covered a meeting of the Quebec Police Commission in which a government witness accused a local businessman of being in league with organized crime. The witness, speaking before a quasi-judicial body, was immune from prosecution for libel, but the reporter was not. When the witness' quote was carried in the paper, the businessman sued—and the paper paid $50,000 in damages for the privilege of learning how meager its privilege really was.

Another area in which U.S. and Canadian law differ is that of fair comment. In the U.S., the courts have ruled that the publication of comment and opinion, as opposed to facts, regarding a matter of public interest should not be hindered, provided that the comment is made "fairly and with honest purpose." The ruling applies to almost any public matter, from a speech by a politician, to a review of a Broadway play by a theater critic, to the opinion of a baseball player about his manager. If the matter is in the public view and has excited legitimate public interest, opinions about it cannot be attacked.

A writer may not say anything factually false about the public matter or public person, but his opinion can be quite wild. An art critic, for example, might say that an artist's paintings look like "the idiot scrawlings of a spastic baboon" and get away with it. He might be sued if he attributed the paintings to someone other than the artist, or if he described a green painting as red, because those would be factual errors. But for his opinion, he is safe as houses.

The U.S. Supreme Court has taken the concept even further. In a 1964 ruling it stated: "When a newspaper publishes information about a public official and publishes it without 'actual malice'—it should be spared a damage suit even though some of the information may not be true." This, the Court said, was to maintain "a profound national commitment to the principle that debate on public issues should be uninhibited, robust and wide-open."

In Canada, the opposite is true. Any false statement made about a public figure, whether it was made with malice or in perfect sincerity, may be grounds for conviction in a libel case. No privilege whatever extends to defamatory comments about a Canadian public figure or personality.

Closely related to the question of fair comment is the concept of the "right to privacy," the right of the ordinary citizen to be left in peace and not hounded by publicity seekers. The statutes in this area are not as well established as those involved in libel and slander, nor backed by as impressive a body of legal precedent, but the possibility that a reporter might be sued for invading someone's privacy is nevertheless real.

In general, the reporter should apply the test of general interest in deciding whether publication of details about a given person's personal affairs might constitute an invasion of privacy. For example, if the President of the United States were an alcoholic (several actually were), publication of the fact would be in the public interest. The President's ability to govern could be affected by his drinking, and the voters have a right to know such things. There might even be a case for claiming that the public has a right to know whether a motion picture star is an alcoholic. The star, after all, is a public figure.

Publishing the fact that Joe Klutz, an assembly-line worker at the Ford Rouge plant, is a problem drinker, however, would not be of any genuine public importance. Klutz would not be a public figure, and any gratuitous attack on his character would injure him to no purpose. The reporter who revealed his problem could be sued for invasion of privacy and would probably lose.

You Raise, I Call

As already noted, only a small percentage of libel suit threats ever get to the courtroom. The vast majority are settled out of court, employing the sometimes elaborate strategies beloved of poker enthusiasts the world over. Reporters, editors, plaintiffs, and their lawyers bluff and counterbluff, hide what's in their hands, and mull their bets until one side or the other finally says: "You raise, I call. Let's see your cards." Sometimes the outcome is predictable, sometimes the whole experience is downright harrowing, but the reporter learns something from each encounter. The author, who has had four or five such run-ins over the course of a career, can testify to that.

Perhaps the first and most comforting thing a reporter learns about libel threats is that most of them don't mean anything. Frequently, the subject of an investigation who is contacted for comment prior to publication of a story will threaten to sue as a form of bluster, an attempt to frighten the reporter away or to prevent him from printing what he knows.

Others, after an unflattering article has appeared, may loudly vow to sue simply to make themselves look good to the public, to play the part of the outraged innocent party. Once their threats have been reported, they have achieved their only real object and promptly drop the matter. Only rarely does anyone go ahead with a suit he knows he cannot win.

When the Montreal *Gazette* discovered evidence in 1974 that a prominent local doctor had been using questionable procedures in his medical practice, the reporter who found the evidence phoned the doctor for comment. "I shall most certainly sue if you print that," the angry doctor told me. He was quite emphatic. The evidence was overwhelming, however, and the doctor even admitted part of what the story charged. Accordingly, the story ran.

No suit ever materialized, but more than a year later I happened to hear a radio broadcast in which one of the doctor's friends was being interviewed. The friend told the talk-show host that the doctor *had* sued the *Gazette* and hinted that he'd won. I was furious, but I became still more angry when I found that the same tale had been given to the editors of a national magazine and that the magazine was telling its readers that we had been "forced to retract" our story.

The doctor's friends were either misinformed as to the facts or lying in order to protect him. The *Gazette's* lawyer was called in, and sharp notices were sent to the radio station and the national magazine. The radio station gave free air time on the same talk show to rebut the doctor's friends, and the magazine sent a written apology and clarification.

The lesson was clear, however. Even when a story stands and no suits are launched, the battle for the truth can still be lost. The reporter has to keep a wary eye open long after publication and be ready to defend a story anywhere. The *Gazette's* story had never been retracted

Maclean's
CANADA'S NEWSMAGAZINE

481 UNIVERSITY AVENUE.
TORONTO. CANADA
M5W 1A7
TELEPHONE (416) 595-1811
NIGHTLINE 595-0222

March 31, 1976

Mr. Thomas F. Pawlick
The Gazette
1000 St. Antoine Street
Montreal, Quebec

Dear Mr. Pawlick,

Thank you for your letter of March 16th. All I can
do is offer you our complete apologies for the letter
written to Mr. Fox casting doubt on your story.

It is particularly embarrassing in view of the fact that
Jim Peters is on our staff and does remember very vividly
the details of your story. Mary Sheppard was not aware
of the fact that Jim was the Gazette's city editor at
the time the story appeared and she asked another ex-
Gazette staffer here who on the paper she could check
on the details of your story so as to answer Mr. Fox.
She was given the name of a Gazette reporter, telephoned
that reporter, and was told that the Gazette had been
forced to retract on the issue of the disposal vacurettes.
In retrospect, it is quite clear that she should have checked
further into the aftermath of your story, but she didn't,
and that led to the unfortunate reply to Mr. Fox.

Mr. Fox's was the only letter we received referring to your
story and I am writing him separately today to explain that
we were totally wrong in saying the Gazette had been forced
to retract it. Needless to say, I am extremely sorry about
the whole affair and have taken steps to try to ensure that
a similar situation does not occur again.

Best regards,

Mel Morris
Managing Editor

*Sometimes the journalist himself is slandered and must fight to keep his own reputation
clean. In this letter a magazine editor apologizes for telling readers that a newspaper
story had been "retracted" when it had not.*

or even seriously questioned, but because of the incorrect tale given out by the doctor's friends, journalists across Canada *thought* the paper had been wrong.

A similar scenario followed the black market adoptions story described in Chapter VI. After the story appeared, the heads of Agency Y and Agency X both threatened to sue the paper and were quoted in other news media to that effect. The lawyer who had cited a $500 fee for arranging a local adoption also threatened to sue and actually went so far as to file papers with the court. He did not press the matter, however, and the suit was eventually dropped without a settlement.

The fact that neither of the agency owners ever filed suit, and that the lawyer's half-hearted attempt was never followed through, was lost on many members of the reading public. Years later, persons recalling the stories in casual conversation still say: "You got burned on that one, eh? How much did you have to pay in damages?" Patiently I explain that I paid nothing, that no damages were assessed because there never was a lawsuit. There was only a threat, voiced in competing news media.

But the threat did its job well.

The fact that we had been obliged to print the clarification notice described in Chapter VI probably had a lot to do with giving the public the wrong impression. The notice said only that the lawyer was not a member of an *international* baby-selling ring, that any questionable adoptions he arranged were strictly local. But even admitting that much was tantamount in some readers' eyes to admitting that the whole story was false. Those two crucial paragraphs cut in the composing room proved costly indeed.

Still another threat surfaced following publication in *Harrowsmith* of the wild-rice stories described in Chapter XI. The libel threat itself was rather clumsy, but several days and many long-distance calls to the magazine's lawyers were required to settle it.

Part of our difficulty was caused by the fact that one of our lawyers was overly timid, fretting and fussing over each detail as if we were involved in a murder charge. Unlike the Montreal *Gazette's* libel lawyer, a hard-nosed scrapper named Keith Ham, this attorney seemed to have adopted the stance from the start that the magazine was wrong and the law firm's job was only to minimize the inevitable damage.

Everything in the story had been meticulously documented, but the lawyer was so thoroughly rattled that it was hard not to succumb to such infectious panic. Part of the reason for such fear may have been the fact that the attorney was young and relatively inexperienced.

The whole flap began when a letter arrived at the magazine from a northern Ontario law firm that had been retained by the wild-rice entrepreneur whose friendship with a provincial cabinet minister had figured prominently in our story. It was a fairly typical lawyer's letter, properly indignant:

"The articles are libelous and in the opinions of my clients and our firm, through facts which are wrong or misstated, and in the innuendo which runs through both articles, they have been defamed. We cannot see how the articles could be published either in good faith or on a misapprehension of the facts. . . . Notice is therefore given pursuant to the Libel and Slander Act of Ontario of the intention of [the clients] to seek damages for libel as a result of these articles."

The true weakness of their clients' case was given away, however, in the next sentence, noting that: "In mitigation of damages, we would ask that you consider either of the following: (1) a printed retraction, or (2) unedited publishing of the attached response [by the plaintiff] in a conspicuous place in your magazine."

In other words, the indignant clients would be perfectly satisfied if we would simply allow them to get a word in edgewise in the form of a letter to the editor, something we would normally be happy to do without any prodding from a lawyer. Any experienced journalist reading such a letter would have seen that the attorney for the cabinet minister's friend wasn't making much of a threat. It was more of a plea for equal time.

To the panicky young lawyer defending us, however, it was all but the end of the world. In a seemingly endless series of telephone calls, we were asked to document virtually every comma and semicolon in every paragraph at issue.

Told that one statement was backed by a taped telephone interview with a witness and a quotation from a published reference book, the lawyer was not satisfied. We had to call the same witness all over again, ask the same questions, and be sure that the reference book was the most recent edition available. Informed that the articles' references to a loan granted to the plaintiff were backed up by photocopies of documents obtained from the Land Registry Office, the lawyer demanded that the loan grantors themselves be telephoned and personally questioned.

Our stories had stated that the entrepreneur in question held permits to harvest rice on close to 2,000 lakes, ponds, and waterways, a fact which he disputed. We had to go to the map room of a local university, pull out charts of the area in question, and actually count every lake, pond, and waterway involved. There were *more* than 2,000, the weary counters discovered.

In the end we were able to back up every point in question with two or more sources, but the attorney still was not happy. The magazine was prepared to print the angry entrepreneur's letter, along with an

editorial reply rebutting each of his claims, but the attorney pessimisti-
cally advised:

"As I am sure you understand, it is essential that every single fact
in this reply be absolutely accurate including any innuendo therein,
otherwise if an action is brought, *Harrowsmith* could be accused of
malice aggravating any damages. . . . Because *Harrowsmith* is published
less frequently than every 31 days, it is not a 'newspaper' within the
meaning of the Libel and Slander Act and therefore, does not get the
protection of s. 5(2) of that Act, whereby a plaintiff is restricted to
his actual damages only. In other words, even by printing a retraction
and apology, [the plaintiff] is not limited to his actual damages."

Such unremitting gloom had by this time begun to have an effect
on even the hitherto confident editors' morale. We began doubting ourselves: "Was the lawyer right, after all? *Should* we apologize? No, it
can't be. We have the proof!" We would probably have ended up in
a state of nervous collapse, the attorney running around us like a manic
chicken shouting "The sky is falling," if the angry entrepreneur had
not jumped the gun at this point and blown it for himself.

Unwilling to wait for the end of the legal sparring to see whether
we would publish his letter, he sent a copy of it to his hometown
newspaper—and they published it, unedited, with no attempt to get
our side of the controversy. The letter was so strident and emotional
that a good case could be made for charging that he was libeling *us.*
I leaped on this possibility and suggested to the lawyer that we might
have grounds for a countersuit of our own. The magazine's publisher
saw the potential immediately and agreed that we should use such a
threat as a defense.

Shortly afterward the entrepreneur's lawyer agreed—with surprisingly little difficulty—to drop the idea of suing us. A waiver was signed
negating any future right to bring such a suit and dropping the earlier
demand for a retraction. All we were asked to do in return was publish
a short notice stating that the entrepreneur in question had not done
anything "improper" or illegal. The plantiff's letter was never run,
and we did not retract a word of our stories.

We could probably have obtained the same result right at the start
by simply telling the entrepreneur's lawyer to take a hike when his
original letter arrived. Our mistake was in letting our own attorney's
case of nerves weaken our self-confidence.

Hindsight vs. Foresight

Where libel is concerned, of course, hindsight is always more accurate
than foresight. It is easier to look back on a past incident and criticize

those involved than to come up with the right answers on the spot, in the heat of battle.

Perhaps the best attitude was that maintained by Montreal libel lawyer Keith Ham, a keen courtroom competitor wise in the ways of the public arena. "My job is to get stories into the paper, not keep them out of it," he once told a worried editor. "If you held back everything that might somehow be actionable, there wouldn't be anything in the paper but the ads—and I'm not even sure about some of them!"

He was a careful man, but he knew that it doesn't pay to be *too* careful.

Chapter XIII

FUTURE FILE

Even the most shocking or important investigative story can produce no impact if it isn't published, and the number of daily newspaper outlets where such stories might appear has dwindled steadily as ownership in the news industry becomes more and more concentrated.

At the beginning of the twentieth century, many of North America's largest cities boasted a dozen or more daily papers, all battling fiercely in the crowded marketplace. Their number and diversity provided outlets for a wide variety of opinion. As late as 1960 there were still eight dailies in New York City and five in Chicago.

Today, there are only four dailies left in New York and three (including the *Wall Street Journal* Midwest edition) in Chicago. Whereas most dailies were once independently owned by local investors, by 1967 half of the daily papers in the United States were chain-owned and nine out of ten of all daily papers were monopolies, that is, papers with no competition in the cities in which they were published. By 1979 fully 97 percent of the 1,544 American cities with daily papers were one-paper towns, and three out of every four newspaper readers were reading a paper owned by a corporate chain.

A similar pattern is found in Canada, where in a single 12-hour period in 1980 both the Winnipeg *Tribune* and the Ottawa *Journal* were abruptly closed, leaving a virtual newspaper monopoly in each of those cities—for the Southam chain in Ottawa and for Thompson Newspapers in Winnipeg. On the same day, Thompson Newspapers sold its Vancouver interests to Southam, confirming a Southam monopoly in the city. Closure of the Montreal *Star* a year earlier had already left Southam's Montreal *Gazette* without an English-language competitor.

As *Canadian Consumer* magazine put it at the time: "The sharp decline in the number of voices providing us with information is one that has been discussed at some length. Less notice has been taken of the fact that in the less competitive situation, a newspaper need not be so diligent in seeking out the news or in serving the community— so there is also an effect on quality. . . . The monopolist in Winnipeg, Ottawa, or Vancouver no longer needs to compete so aggressively on

135

the technological front, nor does he need to be so innovative in trying to serve the reader/consumer."

As *Esquire* magazine has noted, dissecting the effect of chain ownership on newspaper quality: "Front pages tend to look alike, editors tend to run the same kinds of stories in the same ways to attract the same kinds of readers, and publishers tend to follow similar promotion, advertising, and circulation strategies."

Such an environment can be very unhealthy for the investigative reporter. Not only are the profit-oriented, libel-shy corporate dons operating his own paper unlikely to welcome controversial stories, but the competing paper where he might once have farmed out a story under a pen name, or whose rival beat man he might have tipped, probably no longer exists. It has gone the way of the Detroit *Times,* New York *Herald Tribune,* and Montreal *Star.* If his own editors refuse to print a story, there is nowhere else to go with it.

Having worked in many one-paper towns, as well as in major cities with several competing dailies, this author has seen the difference firsthand. At the Detroit *News* tips were acted upon immediately, and the appearance in the rival Detroit *Free Press* of a story we did not have was cause for strenuous efforts to match or better the story. The opposite was true of the paper in a one-paper town. Hot news tips sometimes went unchecked for days or weeks, and in-depth features and investigations were deemed "too much hassle to bother with."

Even more troubling to those concerned with the future of investigative journalism is the tendency of the boards of directors of corporate newspaper chains to include members who also sit on the boards of companies whose activities their own newspapers are supposed to report.

In its December 1979 issue, the *Columbia Journalism Review* reported that "most of the 290 directors of the 25 largest newspaper companies are tied to institutions the papers cover." The *Review* added that "conflict of interest among this group, the directors, is not yet widely perceived as a problem . . . despite the fact that a year-long study of nearly 300 directors of the nation's largest newspaper companies shows thousands of interlocks."

Thus, as already noted in Chapter VIII, the board of the New York *Times* included former Pennsylvania Governor William Scranton and U.S. Energy Council member William F. May. The *Times'* editors may have been perfectly truthful in saying that the presence of these two men on the board had no influence on their paper's coverage of the nuclear accident at Three Mile Island, but the potential was there.

As the number of daily newspapers becomes smaller and smaller, and those that remain are taken over by chains whose officers are far from impartial, the quality and frequency of investigative stories could drop drastically.

Coverage of important regional and rural stories is also likely to suffer as the number of independent, locally owned publications declines. The large urban daily, which increasingly sets the tone for the rest of the papers in a state or province, frequently has blinders on when it comes to covering events beyond the geographical limits of suburbia.

This was the case in Michigan, where nearly nine million people were poisoned after a chemical fire retardant, PBB, accidentally contaminated cattle feed in the early 1960's. The poison entered the food chain when the cattle ate it, contaminating their meat and milk, but not until virtually every resident of the state had been affected and the damage already done did the Michigan daily papers take the story seriously.

As Joyce Egginton noted in her book, *The Poisoning of Michigan:* "It was a long time before any Michigan editor was persuaded that there was a story worth chasing down dirt roads not even marked on the state's highway map."

The same kind of urban myopia exists in nearly every state and Canadian province.

Grounds for Optimism

Despite such discouraging trends, there are grounds for optimism on the future of investigative journalism.

To begin with, the decline in diversity among daily newspapers has been accompanied by a corresponding rise in the number and variety of magazines and weekly papers. In the "movement years" of the 1960's and early 1970's, when civil rights, women's liberation, the environment, and the war in Vietnam became the focus of energetic protest groups, hundreds of local "underground" papers and magazines sprang up to fill in the gaps in the often biased, pro–status quo reporting of what became known as the "establishment press."

Many of these underground, or alternative, publications died young when the war ended and the Nixon administration fell. For lack of a solid set of issues, they succumbed to triteness and posturing. The best of them, however, survived and have become part of the accepted scene in journalism. These include such publications as *Rolling Stone, The Village Voice, Rain,* and *Harrowsmith,* all of which frequently carry investigative articles of high quality and reliability.

Mother Jones, founded in 1976, is a magazine devoted entirely to in-depth investigative reporting. Though heavily biased in favor of the political left, its exposés and news breaks are often far ahead of the rest of the media. Sometimes *Mother Jones* is the only publication with nerve enough to break a story. The magazine's philosophy comes through loud and clear in its own promotional material:

"Do you suppose Thomas Jefferson believed that airbrushed center-fold nudes, CIA news plants or corporate-dominated media would protect the public from power-hungry politicians, arbitrary judges and venal business executives? And when our ancestors struggled to protect a free press, do you suppose they envisioned slick magazines full of celebrity photos, inane gossip, half-digested news, establishment commentary and ruling class opinions?

"We doubt it. We think they hoped for hard-nosed independent investigation, incisive political analysis, cultural criticism and good old American satire. So we started *Mother Jones.*"

Other magazines that often carry well-researched investigative stories include *The Nation, Washington Monthly, Esquire,* and *Harpers.*

Frequently, weekly newspapers are the best place for an exposé to be broken. Occasionally trade journals blow the lid on their own industries. In the PBB poisoning case mentioned earlier, it was a weekly trade journal, the *Michigan Farmer,* that broke the story and kept plugging at it until the other media noticed. The journal had the courage to keep digging out the facts even after the Michigan Farm Bureau, angered by the stories, canceled $45,000 worth of annual advertising in the journal.

The effect achieved by the work of even one responsible publication is sometimes startling. As noted in Chapter VIII, the "Silent Toll" stories in *Harrowsmith* were picked up by newspapers and radio stations all over North America and the world and even translated into Japanese. More than a year after the stories appeared, the magazine was still receiving calls from persons across the continent seeking extra copies or further information on what we reported.

Those in industry and government who are exposed in investigative stories may supply further testimony to a single article's value. For example, an article on dangerous food additives published in *Harrowsmith* in 1979 prompted a confidential memo to be circulated among members of the Grocery Products Manufacturers of Canada (an industry group). Written by the GPMC vice-president, the memo warned:

"[The article] is based on at least 20 hours of interviews. . . . It brings together all the major current concerns on food safety in a relatively balanced and well reported fashion. There are some minor errors, more in emphasis than in fact, but essentially it gives a fair reflection of how Dr. [Alexander] Morrison views the world—a balanced statement of concern by a distinguished scientist with the responsibility for public health aspects of the food industry in Canada.

"It is not felt desirable to respond to the editors of *Harrowsmith* on this article, since this would give it more prominence. However, it is possible that the article may trigger some further media coverage and to guard against this a GPMC position statement is in course of preparation."

This statement, warning that a "balanced, well reported" article should not be given "prominence," speaks for itself.

In addition to the variety of magazines and weekly papers willing to print investigative work, journalists interested in doing in-depth reporting may glean encouragement from the existence of several professional and educational groups formed to reinforce and improve the quality of investigative journalism.

In the United States, the murder of Arizona newsman Don Bolles in the early 1970's so outraged his fellow reporters that a spontaneous "task force" of experienced investigative writers was formed and sent to Arizona to finish what Bolles had been unable to complete before his death. The group spent months digging into every aspect of the state's corrupt political machine, the same machine Bolles was getting close to when a bomb planted in his car by a hired killer exploded. The task force's stories, printed in papers across the country, laid bare Arizona's sins and served notice that the reporting fraternity would support its own.

This initial group subsequently evolved into a permanent organization, the U.S. Investigative Reporters and Editors, Inc. A similar group, the Center for Investigative Journalism, was formed in Canada in 1978 by the Montreal *Gazette's* Henry Aubin and several other reporters. The two groups hold conventions, sponsor workshops, and in general attempt to aid members who are trying to produce quality work in an industry where quality all too often is a thing of the past.

Another group whose efforts have proven valuable to journalists is Ralph Nader's Center for Study of Responsive Law, which held its First Annual Student Conference on Investigative Reporting in 1981. The conference included talks and workshops by reporters from the Washington *Post, Rolling Stone,* Jack Anderson's group, the New York *Times, The Progressive, The Village Voice,* and television's *60 Minutes.*

Especially since the Watergate scandals—uncovered through the investigative work of reporters from the Washington *Post* and Los Angeles *Times*—the journalism departments of many colleges and universities have also given greater emphasis in their courses to investigative techniques.

In short, the future of investigative journalism in the United States and Canada is far from bleak. On the contrary, given the North American commitment to free speech and freedom of the press, this continent is probably the best place in the world for an investigative journalist to work, and will likely remain so.

Chapter XIV

A MUCKRAKER'S LIBRARY

A book based chiefly on the experiences of one person cannot hope to adequately cover such a broad topic as that of investigative journalism. At best, it can only serve as an introduction to the subject, encouraging serious reporters to continue their own education through further reading and—of far greater importance—their own experience on the street.

The following bibliography, based on fifteen years' background in the news industry, should help set the newcomer on the right route.

Information on Investigative Techniques, Style, and Problems

Mitford, Jessica. *Poison Penmanship.* Vintage Books, New York, 1980.

Written by the "queen of the muckrakers," this book recounts the author's adventures while investigating the Famous Writers School, the North American funeral industry, and other strange entities. A lively exposition of how Mitford got the goods.

Edelhertz, Herbert. *The Investigation of White-Collar Crime: A Manual for Law Enforcement Agencies.* U.S. Government Printing Office, Washington, D.C., 1977.

An explanation of the methods and issues involved in investigating white-collar crime.

Jackson, R. L., editor *Criminal Investigation.* Sweet and Maxwell, London, 1962.

The standard work on criminal investigation, used as a basic text by police forces all over the world.

Midwest Academy, Inc. *Open the Books—How to Research a Corporation.* Chicago, 1974.

A guide to the basics of ferreting out financial, stock ownership, and other information on corporations.

A Citizen's Guide on How to Use the Freedom of Information Act and the Privacy Act in Requesting Government Documents. U.S. Government Printing Office, Washington, D.C., 1977.

Despite its overlong title, this booklet is a worthwhile guide showing how to use U.S. laws to obtain government records. Includes a list of selected government agencies.

How to Read a Financial Statement. Merrill, Lynch, Pierce, Fenner & Smith, New York, 1975.

A layman's guide to deciphering corporations' annual reports.

Wittenberg, Philip. *Dangerous Words.* Columbia University Press, New York, 1941.

A classic exposition of the ins and outs of libel law in the United States.

Hamilton, E. Douglas. *Libel: Risks, Rights, Responsibilities.* MacMillan, New York, 1966.

An in-depth discussion of libel law, aimed at the working newsman and woman and including more recent jurisprudence than Wittenberg's study.

Crossley, David J., and Wilson, Peter A. *How to Argue.* Random House, New York, 1979.

A good introduction to the art and science of logical—as opposed to merely emotional—argument, outlining the rules of logic as practiced by debaters throughout history.

Domenach, J. M. *La Propagande Politique (Political Propaganda).* Presses Universitaires de France, Paris, 1962.

An excellent description of the dishonest techniques used by political propagandists from Adolf Hitler to Madison Avenue's hucksters.

Lewis, Roger. *Outlaws of America.* Pelican Books, Middlesex, England, 1972.

A short popular history of the so-called underground press that sprang up in North America and England during the Vietnam War years and managed to publicize issues ignored in the "establishment" press.

Sinclair, Upton. *The Jungle.* Published by the author, 1906.

A documentary novel describing conditions in Chicago's stockyards at the turn of the century, this book is widely regarded as the pioneer effort in "muckraking" investigative journalism. It has become a classic, available in several editions.

Columbia Journalism Review, 200 Alton Place, Marion, Ohio 43302.

Published under the auspices of the Columbia University Graduate School of Journalism, this monthly magazine is the conscience and critic of the newspaper industry in North America, containing articles that weigh the performance, good or bad, of the media.

The Writer, 8 Arlington Street, Boston, Massachusetts 02116.

A monthly magazine containing excellent how-to articles on writing and selling stories to newspapers and magazines. Each issue contains a detailed listing of current freelance markets and their requirements.

Writer's Digest, 9933 Alliance Road, Cincinnati, Ohio 45242.

A monthly magazine similar to *The Writer,* but with less extensive market lists. All three of the above-mentioned magazines are carried in public libraries.

Freelance Market Lists

Brady, John, and Schemenaur, P. J. *Writer's Market.* Writers Digest Books, Cincinnati, Ohio, 1981.

Published yearly, this book gives a comprehensive list of newspaper, magazine, and book publishing markets for writers in both the U.S. and Canada.

Goodman, Eileen. *The Canadian Writer's Market.* McClelland & Stewart Ltd., Toronto, 1976.

Fulton, Len, and May, James Boyer. *Directory of Little Magazines and Small Presses.* Paradise, California. Published yearly. Gives names and addresses of underground and alternative publications that may publish stories rejected elsewhere.

Professional Groups for Journalists

Investigative Reporters and Editors, Inc., P.O. Box 868, Columbia, Missouri 65205.

Headquartered at the University of Missouri Columbia School of Journalism, the IRE provides aid, information, and encouragement to those involved in investigative projects.

The Centre for Investigative Journalism, Box 571, Victoria Station, Montreal, Quebec H3Z 2Y6 Canada.

Publishers of the *CIJ Bulletin,* this is the Canadian equivalent of the U.S. Investigative Reporters and Editors, Inc. The center makes grants available to journalists unable to obtain sufficient funds elsewhere to complete investigative projects.

The Fund for Investigative Journalism, Room 1021, 1346 Connecticut Ave. NW Washington, D.C. 20036.

Operated by Howard Bray, the fund provides grants-in-aid to journalists working on worthwhile investigative stories.

How the Real World Works: Selected Titles

Mintz, Morton, and Cohen, Jerry. *America, Inc.* Dell Publishing Co., New York, 1972.

Documented descriptions of how large corporations dominate the political and economic life of the U.S.

Green, Mark J., and Fallows, James M. *Who Runs Congress?* Bantam Books, New York, 1972.

An exposé of how special interest groups, from Big Business to Big Labor, influence how America's elected representatives vote.

Kennedy, Robert F. *The Enemy Within.* Popular Library, New York, 1960.

The late Senator Robert Kennedy's classic memoir of his battle with the Teamsters Union and its leader, the late James R. Hoffa.

Marchetti, Victor, and Marks, John D. *The CIA and the Cult of Intelligence.* Dell Publishing Co., New York, 1974.

The Central Intelligence Agency exposed by one of its former agents.

Bernstein, Carl, and Woodward, Bob. *All the President's Men.* Warner Paperback Library, New York, 1975.

The inside story of the Watergate scandal that brought down President Richard Nixon, told by the reporters who broke the story.

Royko, Mike. *Boss: Richard J. Daley of Chicago.* Signet Books, New York, 1971.

How an old-fashioned, big-city political machine works, by a Pulitzer Prize-winning reporter.

Croft, Roger. *Swindle: A Decade of Canadian Stock Frauds.* Gage Publishing Co., Toronto, 1975.

How clever crooks took investors for several of the worst rides in stock market history.

Keene, M. Lamar. *The Psychic Mafia.* Dell Publishing Co., New York, 1976.

How spurious spiritualists take fortunes from the credulous.

Gibson, Walter B. *The Bunco Book.* Sidney Radner, Holyoke, Massachusetts, 1946.

The rackets of con men and carnival grifters exposed in humorous fashion.

Carey, Mary and Sherman, George. *A Compendium of Bunk.* Charles C. Thomas, Springfield, Illinois, 1976.

A handbook for fraud investigators explaining how con-games work.

Talese, Gay. *Honor Thy Father.* Fawcett Publications, New York, 1971.

A *New York Times* reporter recounts the life of the Bonnano Mafia family.

Maas, Peter. *Serpico.* Bantam Books, New York, 1973.

What happens in too many big cities when an honest cop tries to do his job.

O'Callaghan, Sean. *The White Death.* College Notes and Texts, Inc., New York, 1967.

How the heroin trade operated in the 1960's.

Robertson, Frank. *Triangle of Death.* Corgi Books, London, 1978.

The story of the Triads—the Chinese Mafia.

Plate, Thomas. *Crime Pays.* Ballatine Books, New York, 1975.

A description of how various rackets, from car theft to truck hijacking, work and how much they pay their practitioners.

Litchfield, Michael, and Kentish, Susan. *Babies for Burning.* Serpentine Press, London, 1974.

How privately owned abortion agencies *really* work.

Van den Bosch, Robert. *The Pesticide Conspiracy.* Anchor Books, New York, 1980.

How dangerous chemical poisons find their way into the food chain through the greed and lack of social conscience of chemical corporation executives.

Bequai, August. *White-Collar Crime.* Lexington Books, Lexington, Mass., 1978.

An excellent description of corporate criminals in action.

Aubin, Henry. *City for Sale.* Editions L'Etincelle, Montreal, 1977.

How big-time foreign investors buy and sell cities, paving the way for urban blight.

Sternglass, Dr. Ernest J. *Secret Fallout.* McGraw-Hill, New York, 1981.

How government and industry have covered up the evidence that radiation is wreaking havoc on the environment.

Opinions on the quality of any publication are bound to be biased, but in the author's view the best investigative reporting being done today can be found in the following newspapers and magazines:

Le Canard Enchâiné, Paris, France.

Mother Jones, San Francisco, California.

The Washington Post, Washington, D.C.

Rolling Stone, New York, N.Y.

Harrowsmith, Camden East, Ontario, Canada.